Heaven
Help Us!

Dear Anne,
2012
Sometimes on this journey called motherhood we have to laugh to keep from crying!
We have Maggie for that! Thanks for being
a wonderful, fun mom to Halle + Maggie.
love, mom

Heaven Help Us!

A Humorous Look at Womanhood

Kari J. Rich

Covenant Communications, Inc.

Cover image: *The Responsible Woman* © 2010 James C. Christensen, © The Greenwich Workshop®, Inc.
www.greenwichworkshop.com

Cover design copyright © 2012 by Covenant Communications, Inc.

Published by Covenant Communications, Inc.
American Fork, Utah

Printed in the United States of America
First Printing: March 2012

18 17 16 15 14 13 12   10 9 8 7 6 5 4 3 2 1

ISBN 978-1-60861-872-9

To Jason—
for love, for laughs, forever

Acknowledgments

SPECIAL THANKS TO MY PARENTS for having no creative writing ability themselves because they passed it all on to me. You supported me, encouraged me, and raised me to do things more like you than I wanted to. Love to Madison, Ivy, and Scott for giving me plenty of fodder for writing and filling my life with learning and laughter. Thanks to Louise Hurd for being the first person to teach me to use and love words. And a special thank you to Jason for being quiet, meek, and private, and for loving and supporting someone who is not.

Foreword/Warning

THIS IS NOT A SELF-HELP book. I don't have all the answers about life or motherhood, but I do have a bunch of goofy experiences. I decided to write them down so that someday when my children come visit me in my old age and they find me eating ruffles off of blankets, it will all make sense.

I was a capable person, I thought. I finished college, got a decent job where I behaved fairly professionally, married a nice guy . . . and furnished our first apartment with banana chairs I stole from a charity drop-off. That should have been my first clue—the banana chairs.

My mother used to wear a muumuu around the house. It had bursting gargantuan fluorescent flowers everywhere and an excess of pleats. I'm sure even Hawaiians would have been offended. As a kid, I loathed "The Muumuu." I writhed in pain if she answered the door in it. And when she answered the phone in it, I was sure those flowers could penetrate phone lines. It was ghastly, a symbol of surrendering personal pride. I knew being a mom was hectic, but I thought some level of dignity could be maintained amid the chaos. Some mothers scrounged around in sweats—that was acceptable—and I decided that was the lowest I would stoop when I was a mother. I would never even own a muumuu when I was a mother. I would maintain dignity in motherhood, maybe even be hip.

Then three children later, on a wintry day, I found myself scampering out the front door barefoot in a magenta, floral, polka dot, XL muumuu, trying to catch my naked toddler before he made another snow angel in the neighbor's yard. The neighbor pulled out of his driveway, and before I could think, I waved at him, as if standing in the knee-deep snow of his yard in a muumuu with a frothing toothbrush hanging out of my mouth and my son taking a leak on his snowman was a perfectly normal scene.

Then it struck me. I was my own worst nightmare—a dignity-impaired Muumuu Mom! No one tells you the afterbirth is really a piece of your brain.

The funny thing is, I bought the muumuu years before as part of a gag costume for a Halloween party. I mingled around the party, causing hysterical laughter as I told about my childhood scars from my mother's muumuu. I didn't know I had really come to the party as the Statue of Irony.

I don't even know how the muumuu escaped from the depths of the Halloween box and became a staple in my wardrobe. It just gravitated toward me. So that's what this book is about—my transmutation to muumuu mommyness. I thought others might relate and laugh with me. Or maybe not relate at all and be totally freaked out that people like me are allowed to procreate.

Table of Contents

1
HMOs Are Not Mother Friendly

I KNOW WHAT HMO REALLY stands for: "Helpless Mother Oppressors" or "Hate Mothers Openly." These titles are much more fitting for the acronym that causes internal bleeding when I hear it. Whoever invented "managed care" lives on The Island of Adults Only because nothing about a child's life, and therefore, a mother's life, is "managed."

As mothers, we pretend in small increments, especially in front of people we want to like us, that our lives and our children are manageable. We smile at croissant luncheons and cross our legs decently, but the truth lurks behind the snag in our panty hose. Those luncheons become interesting when we chuck the croissants, pull out the Hostess boxes, and exchange war stories. Every mom should laugh hard enough to test postpartum bladder control once in a while.

We laugh because every mother knows "managed care" goes totally against real mommy life. Kids don't get sick during "open hours." They get sick or injured during "emergency/outpatient clinic hours" when patching up costs more. My child can jump off a five-story building into a land mine camouflaged with boulders and thorn bushes and walk away scar-free during open hours. But somehow, at three in the morning, she can simply roll over her doll and dislocate her shoulder—my daughter's, not the doll's.

Stomach flu never originates during the day at our house. My children have to be in a deep sleep. I have to be in a deep sleep. It's winter, our beds piled with cozy extra blankets. Then it comes—the sound, the sound that occurs in the background of your dream, making your dream persona say, "What's that recurring sound? It doesn't fit this story." Then the real you wakes up abruptly with full knowledge of what that sound means.

It's the sound of the washing machine going nonstop for three days. It's the sound of tub water running at 2 a.m. mixed with the uncontrollable cries of a child getting vomit washed out of her hair. It's the sound of a sibling screaming in tired delirium because "that's so gross, and now it stinks in here!" It's the sound of a tired couple hurling unreasonable blames, like, "Why did you feed her spaghetti? You know it stains!"

Where are HMOs on such a night?

Ring, ring, ring. Click. "I'm sorry, we're *closed*. Please call back during our brief and inconvenient regular hours or visit your nearest emergency/outpatient clinic for assistance for only triple the cost, and thank you for choosing our HMO because we care—really."

I have a classic HMOMHS (Health Management Organization Mommy Horror Story). It's Sunday morning. I'm frantically getting my kids ready for church while my husband is at a meeting. I'm trying to fulfill a New Year's resolution to be on time for church, even though it's March and I haven't succeeded yet. I was doing one daughter's hair while my other daughter experimented with how far up her leg she could make a run in her tights go. (I categorize tights as disposable.) My son escaped outside to check driveway puddle levels when my husband drove up to get something he'd forgotten.

While I gathered materials for a teaching assignment, my husband attempted to herd our brood into the minivan. We lived two blocks from the church and drove two cars there every week. My son was toddling down the garage stairs, holding his dad's hand, when he tripped. Out of instinct, my husband pulled up on his arm to catch the fall.

I arrived on the scene as Jason, my husband, was buckling our bawling son into his car seat. Jason explained that he hadn't fallen or bumped anything, so he couldn't figure out why he was still crying. Maybe it just scared him. He kissed me for luck and zoomed off. I pulled out of the garage with my van full of screaming demons and waved at my neighbor, Malibu Barbie, who was basking in the Jacuzzi on her deck and sipping a chilled beverage. I was, by the way, running on time. Not that it would matter.

When I tried to get my son out of the van, he bellowed in pain any time I touched his arm. Based on the explanation of the incident, I deduced that a joint had slipped out of socket. I knew there was probably some simple procedure to pop it back in, but I didn't know it, and I didn't want to risk tarnishing his pitching career. So I hauled my yelping papoose into the church, retrieved my daughters out of the drinking fountain, and hunted the halls for my husband.

One of my neighbors stopped me in the hall. "Are you looking for your husband?"

I nodded.

"Does he drive a blue compact car?"

I nodded again.

"I think that's him pulled over by a policeman in front of the church."

I peered out the window. Sure enough, there was a heathen cop issuing my husband a ticket. I started chanting, "What would Jesus do?" in my mind as I searched out some poor soul to dump my children and lesson on. I left my daughters and manual in a pew with a friend and headed for the hospital.

While walking up the icy ramp to the emergency entrance, carrying my sobbing toddler and a weighty diaper bag full of coercion goods, I questioned why I hadn't chucked all my heels out with the first pail full of dirty diapers. I yelled out my name and problem to a nurse in a bulletproof glass booth, and she handed me a novel on a clipboard to fill out. I took a seat and filled out forms as my son cradled his arm and wiped his nose on the last dry-clean-only frock I will ever own.

When I handed the nurse my personal history, she told me it would be about a fifty-minute wait. "Perfect," I said, "then the doctor can check my son's ruptured vocal chords too. Oh, and could he fit me with a hearing aid and a straight jacket, or do I need to fill out another form for that?"

It's a good thing the bulletproof glass works both ways.

The nurse smiled a grotesque smile that could only have been learned at some corporate training meeting about dealing with anti-HMO rebels as she said, "You know, we just opened an off-hours pediatric clinic in the north wing. Since your son's condition isn't serious, you could go there. I think it's cheaper."

Ka-ching! I headed to the north wing. The reason they call these portions of buildings "wings" is that you wish you had some to get there. I turned the final corner to find the waiting room dark and the receiving desk vacant.

I was about to join my son in a howling duet when a nurse stepped through the door. "Are you here to see a doctor?"

"No, I'm here to make a large, generous donation to your organization so I can have the new homicidal mothers wing named after me."

"What?"

"Yes, I'm here to see a doctor."

"Well, we open in thirty minutes, but you can be filling out your paperwork while you wait." She reached for a clipboard.

What would Jesus do? What would Jesus do? What would . . . The nurse must not have liked the color of purple I was turning because she said, "Or you can go to the outpatient clinic in the south pole wing, and they could help you now."

I stepped back from the desk and searched my inner universe for a happy place. "I'll do that."

I started trudging back toward the outpatient clinic like a packhorse carrying the limp kill from a hunt. In the distance, I thought I recognized a pediatrician from my doctor's office. He must be the doctor on duty for the after-hours clinic!

Yes, it was he. He would help me. He would see that my ankles were swollen to the circumference of my thighs, notice my permanently altered posture, take pity on my son, who was now crying in sign language.

"Doctor Smudge, isn't it?" I called out.

"Yes."

"I'm so glad to see you. My son here—his arm slipped out of the socket and—"

"I understand." He took a casual sip from his steaming mug and looked down at his watch. "I can help you in thirty minutes." He walked off.

I stood there, stunned. I had a *Little House on the Prairie* episode flashback. I saw Doc Baker nursing little Carrie back to health in the middle of a stormy winter night and then turning away the Ingalls' offer of their blue-ribbon hen as payment.

"Managed care bites!" I yelled down the hall after him.

A person in the pharmacy across the hall held out a Prozac sample toward me. I stomped off.

"I'm back," I said to the outpatient clinic nurse. "The after-hours clinic opens only after the staff has had a leisurely breakfast."

"Can I help you?"

"I was here before, about my son's arm."

"Oh yeah." She grimaced as her memory betrayed her. "Here, fill this out." She held out a clipboard.

"I already did this paperwork."

"Yeah, but you left, so we put it through the shredder."

At this point, I think I had an out-of-body experience and a hostile alien took over because I cannot account for my behavior, and I think I was speaking in tongues. When I returned to human consciousness, I heard the nurse say, "You know what, we'll just tape your paperwork back together; bring your son around here."

She led me to a three-foot-square curtained partition, where I sat holding my son on a tissue-papered bed for forty-five minutes. I was about to slip into a coma when a being in surgeon-green scrubs pulled back the curtain. "What do we have here?"

Words were difficult. "My son . . . his arm . . . it slipped . . . or something . . ."

"Ah, looks like a common case of nursemaid elbow." He took my son's arm and gently rotated it. We heard a soft popping noise. Midscream, my son stopped cold and smiled.

That soft popping sound cost me ninety minutes of mortality and one hundred and sixty-two dollars and fifty-four cents (not including my husband's traffic ticket). I had barely wrinkled the tissue paper I'd sat on.

"We see this all the time with toddlers," he said jovially as he tousled my son's hair and handed him a dumdum sucker.

"Can I have a sucker too, or does that cost extra?"

He held out the box of suckers. "This one's on the house."

Doc Baker's spirit lives on.

2
The Wendy in Me

I ONCE TOOK MY KIDS to see a new Peter Pan movie. Far from the whimsical cartoon, this was a dramatic, artsy, European fantasy flick. I was mesmerized by chiffon fabrics flowing through starry nights, lyrical accents saying things like, "It's simply lovely, Petah." Captain Hook's evil engulfed the screen as symphonic minor chords accompanied his dastardly deeds. I was submerged in their world, longing to hang out in the lair of the Lost Boys, where hygiene neglect is mandatory as you exist permanently in your pajamas.

Wendy tossed her tresses and flittered around fantasyland in her nightgown, flirting coyly with Peter Pan, the pubescent hottie who used his boyish charm to woo her with the idea of eternal youth. She casually avoided such considerations, basking in the adventures of fancy. But as in all stories, there comes the moment of truth—decision time, Wendy. What should she do?

Peter lured her with sweet talk and ocean blue eyes. "Stay, Wendy. Stay here, and you'll be young forever." Peter was persuasive, dreamland was delish, but Wendy would have to give up her chance to raise her own children, to grow old with a tall, responsible provider with dark hair and a 401K. She looked up at him, pining, teetering on the edge of decision . . .

"Don't be stupid, Wendy!" I burst from my theater seat. "Do you know how much Oil of Olay costs per ounce? Have you seen Walmart's maternity line? Men shrink as they age, you know, all except for their noses and ears, which grow enormous and sprout bushes. Nothing fades stretch marks—infomercials lie. Look at him, Wendy. He's beautiful; so are you. Stay with him . . . stay . . . stay!"

I sank back into my seat, tears rolling out of my crow's-feet. Although the rest of the theater population seemed affected by my words, the voice of reason belted from the balcony did not reach Wendy. Her future fetuses whispered, and she turned her back on foster parenting the Lost Boys with incorrigible Pan. Tragic.

Mothering the Lost Boys offers the perfect guilt-free parenting experience. Their name starts with *lost*, for heaven's sake, so no matter how lousy of a job you do as a mother, it wouldn't be your fault they don't grow up to be doctors and lawyers and such. They'll explain to Oprah how they spent their childhood in the care of an underage loafer who packed a knife in his green tights, carried on an undefined relationship with a fairy, and pestered pirates for kicks. Oprah will gape at the idea and ask, "And where was your mother through all this?" To which the Lost Boys reply, "We didn't have one until Peter brought home some teenage babe in a nightgown."

It's that maternal nudge that sends Wendy, and all of us, back to reality. She wants her own experience of mothering. She sees it like a life insurance commercial—lullaby medley coos behind soft lens montages of baby wrapping her tiny hand around Dad's finger, first steps, laughter, pushes on swings, and so on. Of course, the montage stops before the teenage years, when your premiums skyrocket because death is imminent for you, your teenager, or both.

What Wendy doesn't see—what none of us sees beforehand—are the deleted scenes, like this one . . .

I am lying on my back on a gurney, preparing myself to be hoisted up by an impatient nurse and my husband to take my first postpartum noncatheterered relief session. I require assistance because my legs are still Jell-O-ish from the epidural. My postpartum belly feels the same but will remain in gelatin form indefinitely. My numbness prevents me from feeling that I need to use the restroom, but the nurse assures me that nature calls.

"Take it nice and slow," the nurse counsels as she rushes me to my feet. My husband latches on to my waist, looking as if he could use a relief session himself.

"Now, if you start to feel lightheaded, let me know," the nurse instructs as we lumber to the loo like a six-legged buffalo.

Just as my assistants set me on the commode, I feel my conscious self start to wan. "Look at me, look at me," the nurse spouts sternly, trying to make eye contact with my pupils before they disappear into my forehead.

I hear her voice through a tunnel. "Whatever you do, don't . . ."

Perhaps I made a quick trip to Neverland myself during that brief recess from reality. But while Wendy floated softly back through the nursery window to face the realities of womanhood gradually, I regained consciousness lying semidraped next to the commode, leaking fluids from sundry places. Womanhood was in full bloom, and my Peter Pan had long since vacated.

I would have turned my attention to recapturing decency if it hadn't been for the wash of nausea forcing my lunch back up toward the light. My nurse read the signs. Seeing my prenatal vitamin–enhanced, brunette locks fanned over my right shoulder, she shrieked, "Turn your head!"

She meant "turn your head to the left"—such clarity sparing this situation from taking another step up on the gross-o-meter. As I retched into my hair, my thoughts turned to my husband standing in the doorway—a stunned statue of shock as he witnessed the rawness of the scene. He hadn't breathed out since the tumble from the toilet. I can imagine the only thing worse than experiencing this scenario would be to witness it. There I was, his maiden, his bride, reduced to a mangled mess of sparse hospital gown and regurgitated turkey-on-white sprawled across the tile floor.

You know it's bad when you've grossed out the nurse. This is a person whose entire job is body fluid management and disposal, and yet, there she stood with an expression that matched my husband's. Neither one knew what to clean up first.

Had I not been covered in various forms of goo, I'm sure my husband would have taken me in his arms and reassured me that this was all worth it because we had a beautiful baby girl screaming her guts out in the nursery. I found out later that the reason for my nurse's urgency in getting the circulation in my legs pumping ASAP was pressure coming from her nursery colleagues, who wanted to turn over primary care of "the squealer" to her unfortunate mother pronto.

On cue, an orderly entered the room to do damage control. I suppose I would normally have been embarrassed to be half-naked in front of a strange man, who was now swabbing barf out of my hair, but embarrassment seemed petty at this point.

After I had been swabbed with a thick layer of antibacterial gel and had resumed occupancy of my gurney and gown, I was apparently ready to meet with my breast-feeding instructor. This uninhibited, earthy woman gave a thorough, interactive 4D introduction to the world of nursing. My red-faced daughter, who'd been summoned for the occasion, was finally sleeping between screaming sessions and had little interest in our lesson, and my novice application of the instructor's methods were no help. The quiet, organic woman, who had barely spoken above a whisper as she'd taught the doctrine of nursing, was starting to get a little red-faced herself. Lady le Leche was passionate that this baby and I were not leaving the hospital without a proper and positive nursing experience and took matters into her own hands. I didn't know how to help except to keep still in the stall while the farmer wrestled with the equipment. After several intense minutes, my daughter finally latched on, and we passed breast-feeding 101.

Fewer than twenty-four hours after giving birth, I was released into the world with my new baby and an array of pharmaceuticals to soothe, stimulate, remedy, balm, pad, release, plug, enhance, and reduce every aching, leaking, engorged, stiff part of my forever-altered body.

I am womanhood, Wendy. Hear me roar.

3
Room Mom

LIKE HMO, THE ACRONYM *PTA* has hidden meaning. It all sounds good, helpful, and community building-ish—which it is, when someone else does it. PTA stands for "Plan Time Away"—time away from your home, family, friends, favorite hobbies, and leisure reading. Of course, any friends you have previous to your PTA association scatter like bowling pins when they find out you've been sucked in. Everyone knows PTA operates like Amway—it's all about recruits.

Unless you want to carry the full load of responsibility, you have to find other people to dump on, I mean delegate to. That's why most recruits come from first-time kindergarten moms. They're perfect prey—naïve, eager, even anxious to get involved as they feel that first snip-snip at the apron strings.

That's how I got duped. It started out simply enough—I signed on to be a "room mom." Oh sorry, I mean "room parent." Let's not discourage that hoard of fathers just lining up to bake cupcakes and sing multiplication rock. If we want to be really politically correct, we would call ourselves "room persons," as there is a growing number of elementary-age juvenile delinquents whose parole officers might want to help out. Even then, "room persons" is leaving out those children who are being raised by extraterrestrials, and I have met legal guardians who are definitely from another planet. "Room beings," perhaps? But that would still exclude those parents who exist but fail to show any vital signs. I personally prefer "room mom." It's traditional, catchy, and with all those repetitive o's and m's, it's fun to say.

On my oldest child's first day of kindergarten, I put her on the bus and bawled. She was venturing out of my comfort zone, heading into the cruel dark world of cafeteria food and communal toilets. Would we become strangers with all this time away from each other? Would her favorite snack still be milk and graham crackers when she got home? I had to get involved, let her know I still cared, that I wanted to be part of her life.

Then the flyer came home.

Heading: *Would you like to become a Room Volunteer?* (Aha! The perfect title—no gender, relationship, or species discrimination, and it held the added bonus of subtle guilt-provoking qualities.)

Copy: *Help plan class parties, chaperone field trips, assist with curriculum. Be a part of your child's education! Check below next to the activities you'd like to be part of.*

Check, check, check, check, check, check, check, check, check!

I'll be there for you, honey! I won't let you down!

The PTA is set up with a scrutinizing weeding process. They start out with small assignments to "feel out" the situation. My first assignment was to provide a class snack. This involved three different checks:

1. Dependability Check.

Will she actually follow through? Maybe she's just a wannabe good mom who volunteers for everything then flakes out. (This category suits me on occasion.)

2. Safety Check.

They run your snack through a metal detector, dissect it, and send it to a lab for testing, then take the remains to a remote part of the desert and blow them up.

3. Image Check.

Your child does this check. Worse than flakiness and food tampering is the chance that you would send something stupid. This was my defeat.

The class snack instructions said the snack should be store-bought, with the professional packaging still intact, and sugary snacks were strongly discouraged. Obviously. Kids already arrive at school hopped up on Rockin' Choc-choc-chocolate Frosted Puffies, not to mention the Willy Wonka stash in their desks.

I took no chances. I sent my daughter with a bag of organic, peeled baby carrots, nurtured with love in a garden next to free-range chickens. Three weeks later, I found the unopened, packaged carrot compost in her backpack.

I confronted her. "I love you, sweetheart. Why would you purposely thwart my efforts to make a decent showing for acceptable snack offering?"

"Duh. Carrots are social death, Mom. Why can't I bring a cool snack like Matthew did?"

"What did Matthew bring?" I asked stupidly.

"Super Sour Jaw Jammer Gummies."

"I thought we weren't supposed to send sugary snacks."

"Double duh. They say stuff like that for show. Teachers want us to be happy, if you catch my drift."

"Oh," I said with the same stupidity. First attempt—*unsatisfactory*.

I thought it was over. I was sure I'd be ousted from the society.

No such luck. I didn't know it then, but I should have taken my reject sign and run. But I was still in the virginal stages of the PTA process.

Though I failed class snack, I was given an opportunity to redeem myself. I was assigned to help at the Halloween carnival. This time I was going to make good. First thing, find a cool costume. I decided to skip the traditional evil, ugly witch because my kids would cry typecasting. I wanted to be on the cutting-edge of the kid world, so I surfed the net for Disney characters.

The way-in-charge mom called to give me my responsibility—Bingo. Right on! I resurrected my desktop publishing skills from the career graveyard and hashed out some custom cards. I was even smart enough to know that most Kindergarteners can't read so I made cards using groovy Halloween clip art instead of letters. (I was naïve concerning hyper Ivy League prep preschools.)

I showed up as Jessie the yodeling cowgirl with my cards tucked under my arm and a bag of M&Ms, ready to have some educational bonding time with my daughter.

When I walked through the door, a miniature Cinderella said, "Jessie has red hair, don't you know? You have brown hair."

Typical of a princess; pick on the tomboy.

"Actually, according to Miss Clairol my hair is autumn chestnut with natural highlights. Let me ask you something, princess. Did you know Cinderella becoming a princess was contingent upon her ability to maintain her sweet, humble disposition despite her elevated position in society? And that if she let the whole princess thing go to her head, her crown was given to the first runner-up, and she was doomed to a life of servitude in the royal laundromat? I bet nobody told you that part of the story, did they?"

"Whaaaaaaaa!" Cinderella ran across the gym and into the arms of her mother—the way-in-charge mom. "Mommy, Jessie is being mean to me!"

Cinderella and her evil non-stepmother crossed the gym. "Are you Mrs. Rich?" she said without a wart on her chin. She was dressed as Snow White, of course.

"I wasn't being mean to your daughter. We were just exchanging constructive criticism."

No response, just a pasted-on smile of tolerance for commoners.

I changed the subject. "I'm the Bingo mom."

"Oh. You can set up right over there." She pointed to the table farthest away from hers. "Do you have everything you need, or do you need some help?" Translation—*You reek of incompetence.*

"Thanks, I think I got it." I flipped my non-red hair and went to set up my game. I thought I would win kudos by bringing M&Ms for card markers—letting the kids use a handful during the game, then they could eat them afterward. The whole "chocolate melts in your mouth, not in your hand" thing didn't register in my mind beforehand, so I didn't realize it would become a scene of sticky hand licking, wiping on overpriced costumes, and greedy consumption. I was out of sanitary M&Ms after the first rotation. I was scrounging around on the floor for small pieces of debris I could use as markers when Snow White came to assess the situation.

Thoroughly disgusted, she said, "What are you doing?"

"I ran out of . . . (incompetence showing . . . fabricate lie) I mean, I was just trying to get down on the kids' level so I could see the world from their view." Shmuck on command is my specialty.

No sale. "Here, Mrs. Witch, I mean, Rich. I brought some card markers, just in case." She tossed me an airtight, labeled Tupperware full of pinto beans and swished off in her full gown.

I had a sudden wash of empathy for the dwarfs, especially poor Sloppy. He's probably the one who gave the wicked stepmother the poisoned apple recipe and a map to the cottage.

While setting up for the next set of squirts, I was addressed by a fat Dracula. "Hey, Jessie, how come you used picture cards instead of regular Bingo cards? Do you think we're stupid or something?"

"You know, kid, you can skip this rotation if you want. Go tell Snow White you need an alternative activity. She probably has a trigonometry textbook stashed in her airtight purse."

The rest of the kids gathered around the table. Aside from know-it-all Dracula, this group seemed amiable enough to participate in a novice level activity if it meant treats.

I called out the first card. "Orange witch."

Sponge Bob spoke up. "How come there's an orange witch? Witches aren't orange; they're green."

"Not all green," Strawberry Shortcake corrected. "Only their skin is green. They wear black."

"Not always," the Grim Reaper intervened. "I've seen witches in purple and brown and red and sometimes even—"

"*Orange witch!*" I interrupted, mildly aggressively. "For anybody who wants a shot at winning a bargain bin prize, work with me, and put a bean on the orange witch on your card."

"Speaking of witch," Zorro whispered to Pippi Longstocking.

"Okay, next we have—"

"Hey, Ms. Jessie?" The Incredible Hulk raised his hand. "I have a problem."

"It's okay if you don't have an orange witch; not all the cards . . ." I quickly saw that the Bingo card was not his problem. The Hulk's nose was exploding with pinto beans. Stupid questions always surface in such situations. "Why did you put the beans up your nose?"

Stupid questions are always followed by stupid answers. "I don't know."

"Well, whatever you do, don't sniff—"

Snnnoorrt!

"Arrrggggh!" Another stupid question. "Why did you sniff them farther up your nose?"

Stupid questions are always followed by stupid answers. "I don't know."

The Hulk sprawled across the 1960s gold Formica lunch table as I removed the beans with some tweezers from my cowgirl holster. All the other activities lost their participants as kids conglomerated to watch the wimpy Hulk squeal like a pig during his nostril cleansing.

When I removed what I hoped was the last bean, I said jovially, "I must have missed the part of the story where Jack crawls down the beanstalk growing out of the jolly green giant's nose."

Fat Dracula laughed.

Snow White did not. "Everyone return to your activities, please. He's going to be fine." She whooshed away again, her complexion looking more ruddy than snowy.

The rest of the rotations went fairly well, aside from a fistfight over the last prize when there was a double Bingo. After I broke up the fight and Snow White saved the day with a spare prize she had—just in case—I reassured Scooby-Doo that the blood on his costume looked cool, like he'd just tangled with the monster who was systematically putting the haunted golf course out of business.

As I cleaned up, feeling as deflated as the stack of pool toys in our shed, my daughter came over and softly patted my arm. "Phat tweezer action, Mom."

I didn't know what that meant, but I took it as a compliment, since the sentence didn't contain a "duh."

Though my carnival showing had its low points, I must have received acceptable clearance because I was allowed to help out in the classroom once a week. I realized the first day that this assignment was not for the faint. Teachers are truly underpaid. I worked in the classroom one hour, one day a week, and came home a blubbering mess. It took me three days to recover each time. I think we should start a crusade to bring back legality for administration of the strap and dunce cap.

Since teachers do not have the option to smack naughty kids, I mean, kids who do naughty things, they have to find alternative disciplinary methods. My daughter's teacher was a genius. She taught them this catchy song about being a peacemaker and provided a "peacemaker's rug." Anytime there was a conflict, the involved parties had to sit opposite each other on the rug and talk it out peaceably. I only got sent to the peacemaker's rug once.

I sat down on the fraying carpet sample and scowled back at the opposing party. "So what's your problem?"

"My problem? Mom, you were the one acting like a doof."

Teacher mediation. "Remember, you two, a peacemaker is never accusing."

I tried to refocus my chi. "I was not acting like a doof. We were just doing creative movement, and 'Kumbaya' is a very expressive piece."

My daughter looked desperately up at her teacher, who came in for the save. "Maybe we could just have your mother help with spelling from now on."

My daughter breathed a sigh of relief and smiled. She was on the winning side of the rug this time.

"Is that all right with you, Ms. Kari?"

"Yes, because I am a peacemaker."

"I think you're going to fit in in our classroom just fine. Now, you two shake hands and return to your seats."

Kindergarten is a good place to start for moms. For the most part, the kids are still fairly innocent and gullible. A big smile and excessive excitement in your voice will make them think even the most boring task is going to be fun. This changes with time. They quickly learn to see through the syrup. It happens sometime between second and third grade. But by this time, you're stuck in the PTA like a pig in a luau.

There I stood, in front of my daughter's third grade class, armed with a masterfully planned "Winter Holiday" (unfortunate politically correct nondenominational title) party. I had the room mom thing whipped. I could spew out a class party in my sleep.

The kids were hyper and noisy, so I tried to get their attention, "I need all eyes on me." This prompted several snaggle-toothed, bed-headed boys to violently dig at their eye sockets and then chuck imaginary eyeballs at me. I neglected to realize that, along with their permanent molars, a sarcasm gland was developing.

The teacher gave them a stern recess-is-on-the-line look, and the party began. The kids humored me through some trivial activities, but I could tell they were unimpressed. I lost them somewhere between a How Fat Can Santa Get game and Pin the Nose on Rudolph (although some nose placements did entertain a group of boys). Then I realized the problem. It was Christmas, and the kids hadn't *received* anything yet. Isn't that what it's all about for kids at Christmas? The loot? Well, the party wasn't over yet. What they didn't know was that I had one more trick up my sleeve. The finale—Pass the Present.

When I unveiled a bag full of wrapped gifts, I knew I had them back in the palm of my hand. They were kinnygartners again—wide-eyed, submissive, and greedy.

I explained the rules, emphasizing that in the end everyone gets a gift so not to worry and just have fun.

Then it began.

What started out as a friendly game of gift getting turned into a grade school–sized brawl. Even after the game was over, kids were bartering the useless contents of their desks to try to get the trinket they were cheated out of. One girl simply said, "What a lame gift," and threw her present on the floor. It was a book. Only the nerdiest of room moms would think a book was a good gift, especially compared to a bobblehead Tweety or a Power Pucker jawbreaker. I wished at that moment that I had my father's infamous "Ungrateful Whelp" speech memorized.

In the end, no limbs were lost, the fire department call was cancelled, and except for imaginary eyeballs, nothing was thrown at me, so it was passable. One kid even said, "Thanks, dude," to me, which I think is the highest praise a third grader can give.

Those were the innocent days of class party planning. I didn't realize my days were numbered. I failed to realize I was under surveillance by the PTA intelligence system. Other PTA moms charading as friendly frazzled moms like myself were actually spies sent out to watch and learn. They're the ones who cheerfully plan parties and pass out fluoride with you, all the while preparing to rat you out to their supervisors. They check out new recruits, and if you make a decent showing in the classroom, you get promoted to administration. Actually, the process is officially called "Nomination."

The nomination process goes like this:
PTA President: "Who isn't here?"
Birthday Table Specialist: "Kari Rich."
PTA President: "I nominate Kari Rich as PTA president."
Box Tops for Education Specialist: "I second it."
PTA President: "All in favor say 'I.'"
Sleep-deprived mother majority: "I."
PTA President: "Any opposed say 'Nay.'"
Snow White: "Nay."
PTA President: "By majority vote, Kari Rich is appointed."
Secretary: "Who is Kari Rich?"
PTA President: "I don't know, but find her phone number and call to tell her I'll be over to officially crown her tonight."

There's no swimsuit competition, no evening gown, no interview, and the package of fabulous prizes is a rip-off too. It includes a binder that weighs more than a rhino and that's full of gibberish papers called "by-laws," cheesy flyer templates with "Hurray for Volunteers" in bubble lettering, and a phone list of potential prey. You also get a PTA board full of other wide-eyed suckers who were dumb enough to get involved in the beginning. Together, we probably don't even equal one full night's sleep. But, hey, we were there when our kids needed us! We cared about our kids' education. We passed class snack, class party, and peacemaker powwow and made it to the big time. We're the proud, the few, the logic-impaired, the PTA Board!

Once the inaugural ball is over, the true meaning of PTA is realized, as described in the beginning. The reason I got involved in the PTA was to be part of my children's education. Now I'm so involved in their education I never see my children.

4
Manicure: A Mini Metaphor-On-Life Experience

I DESERVE TO BE PAMPERED occasionally.

My love knows, for he was the giver of the Golden Ticket.

Scheduled escape. Slap on ball cap. Button overalls. Run.

Oops. Run back. Brush teeth.

Run again.

Bound into day spa. Techno-pop blaring. Cosmo cover glaring.

Frumpy, bumpy me. Oh well.

"Meet your nail technician."

Sounds official. What's she going to do to me? Doesn't matter. I'm away.

"Hi. I'm Marasol."

Trendy name. She's hip. I'm hipped.

Oh well. She's official. I'm paid for. Pamper me.

Dig, dig. Scrape, scrape. What's in there?

Don't ask.

Buff, buff.

"What shape would you like your nails?"

More than one nail shape?

"I'll leave that up to 'the technician.'"

Unamused. Buff, buff.

Glop and goo. Rub, rub. Hand massage, Oooooooo. Best part so far.

Rushed. Recognizes the stench of a Golden Ticket holder—non-regular.

Is it the ball cap? Fresh scent of toothpaste midafternoon?

More glop.

"Do you want color?"

"Yes!" Transform me into a hottie.

"Choose."

Rainbow display: green, blue, glitter, purple, dazzle, gold, red, red, red, sparkle.

Contemplate . . . reach . . . grab . . . Natural. Oops, not a hottie color.

Oh well.

Brush, brush. Brush, brush. Brush.

How much goop can fingernails hold?

Done.

"Thanks for letting me do this for you."

Thanks for letting my husband pay you for this.

"Do you want a drink while you dry?"

Does that cost more? Golden Ticket all-inclusive?

Hip enough not to ask.

"Sure, juice." Find out.

Dry, dry. Sip, read, dry.

"You should be plenty dry now." (i.e., "Get out.")

Front counter. Turn in Golden Ticket.

Indication concerning drink?

No indication. No extra charge. Pampered indeed.

Home again, home again, jiggedy jig.

"Hi, Mommy. Pretty nails." Touch, mar, clunk, kiss, streak, hug, slur.

Pampering over.

Scrub, mop, play, comb.

Read, wash, hug, dance, clean.

Chipped, peeled, marred, scarred, rubbed.

Natural, a fossil of real life.

Life is good.

5

Hope for the Directionally Impaired

IN A WORLD OF SUPERSTORES and self-serve, you've gotta love the old-fashioned existence of the grocery store bag boy. Here is a strapping young man who is taking the initiative to join the work force in his youth to save for college or a mission, pay for prom, or reimburse his parents for horrific cell phone overages. He performs menial tasks, like filling bags, loading groceries, and locating abandoned carts from hither and yon in the parking lot, all for menial pay. But through this work, a young man becomes responsible, humble, and skilled.

Some of them are pretty cute too. So when that sixteen-year-old boy flips his blond hair out of his eyes and asks, "Can I help you out to your car, ma'am?" I want to say, "You bet your baby face you can!"

But I can't.

It is always at that moment, when I look into his clear blue eyes, that I realize I have no idea where my car is parked. The last thing I want is some teenage hottie following me aimlessly around the parking lot with my cart full of fibrous cereals and me acting like a senile old bat. Though it breaks my heart to refuse, I would much rather leave the store with Bag Boy Bieber thinking I'm so young and vigorous that I don't need help hefting my roughage out to the car.

Attempting to keep the truth on the down-low and appear young and hip, I reply, "Thanks, dude, but I got it."

Most of the bag boys let me go peacefully out of the automatic double doors with my pride intact. They don't have to see me a few seconds later when tears fill my eyes as I scan the vast parking lot looking for a familiar vehicle. They don't have to watch as I walk up and down the rows, holding my key remote in the air, pushing the button, looking for the flashing lights of my pitiful Momobile. They are spared from the pathetic phone call I make to my husband, asking him to go out to the garage and tell me which vehicle I drove into town. For many years, I was able to keep my shameful secret to myself and preserve the innocence of the beautiful bag boy population.

Until one day a bag boy overachiever pressed the issue.

I was stocking up at the annual case lot sale, and I had gorged on canned goods, large bags of flour, sugar, and other essentials. My cart was busting at the seams, and though the bag boy was a definite trophy and I would have appreciated the help and the eye candy, the visual of me wandering the parking lot like a lab rat in a test maze appeared in my mind's eye, and I gave my usual regrets.

But Bag Boy Tall, Dark & Handsome got all up in my grill, "Really, ma'am. I don't mind." He gestured toward the cart handle I held.

"Thanks anyway." I tried to disguise a grunt as I attempted to move forward.

"Ma'am, it's my job. Let me help you."

At this point, being called "ma'am" started to bug. It stopped feeling respectful and polite and instead made me feel like I was about to star in the sequel to *Steel Magnolias*.

"No, really, it's okay." I hurled my big mama purse around to shove him a little out of the way as I took the cart handle in a death grip.

"Okay, lady. Whatever." He threw his hands up and backed off with a snarky huff.

Lady? That's ma'am to you, you zitty little punk! I decided he wasn't really that cute anyway and leveled myself horizontally with the cart to force movement.

The cart lurched forward abruptly, knocking me off balance. My purse slipped off my arm and splayed its dense personal contents across the filthy floor. A few yards away, a little boy picked up the small pink plastic package that had rolled in front of his feet and exclaimed, "Hey, a prize!" I quickly cut my losses and grabbed what I could.

As I shoved a reading head lamp and an unwrapped piece of gum into my purse, BB TD&H handed me a lidless lipgloss and said, "Just let me help you."

I took it from him and removed a gooey strand of hair. I wouldn't look at him. "I can't."

"You can't? Why not?"

The truth does not set you free, by the way. It just makes you look more pathetic, which is why I rarely use it. But this time I relented. "Because. I have no idea where my car is parked."

In his big brown eyes, I saw eighteen rows of heat-exposed blacktop flash by. Even hot, polite bag boys know when to call it. "Oh."

"Yeah. It's like that. Thanks anyway." I heaved away.

Don't feel sorry for me.

It's not my fault I have no sense of direction. I used to think it was. I used to beat myself up over the fact that every time I walked out of a shop in the mall I exited the same direction I entered and wound up in a shop I'd already been in. I used to get so frustrated with myself when I drove around the six square blocks of the small town I'd lived in for years looking for the friend's house I'd been to a hundred times.

All this self-hate was for nothing because I've figured out why, after living in the same community for twenty years, I am still unable to drive straight to the big university campus, my alma mater, on the first try. It's a scientifically proven excuse—I don't have enough magnetite in my brain.

I know it sounds like a hoax, but it was published in a very reputable publication with scientific sources and everything, so it has to be true. For those of you who don't know, magnetite is "a ferromagnetic mineral with chemical formula Fe_3O_4, one of several iron oxides and member of the spinel group." In short, it is a mineral that contains magnetic properties, and it is present in the human brain—more in some than others, apparently.

Scientists found that people with a strong sense of direction had larger quantities of magnetite in their brains than those of us they picked up to use for the case study when we were wandering around parking lots. Its magnetic property gives the ability to sense the polarity of Earth's magnetic field and works in the brain like a literal "inner compass." Is it any wonder that magnetite is found in the brains of bees and homing pigeons?

Do you know what a relief it is for someone like me to find this out? Do you know what it's like to stare at the New York City subway map in a panic while traveling with your younger sister and have her navigate you out of the seedy neighborhood you accidentally ended up in? And she's a blonde!

I'm not stupid. I'm not senile. I'm not losing my marbles. I'm just missing a few rocks in my head. I think the whole world should be made aware of this important discovery so the stigma surrounding silent sufferers of magnetite deficiency, like myself, can be lifted. They should make one of those medical bracelets for us to wear so when we find ourselves repeatedly entering and exiting the same mall boutique, we can just show our bracelet to the clerks and quell their shoplifter suspicions. After a beautiful bag boy finishes loading my cart, I can just flash him my bracelet and a flirty smile and be on my clueless way.

A great burden has been lifted.

Now I'm just waiting for the discovery of the vitamin deficiency that will explain why I'm always late.

6
Hawk Stalker

I SAW ALFRED HITCHCOCK'S MOVIE *The Birds* when I was fifteen years old. I was at a party, and one of only a few people without someone to smooch, so I actually watched the movie. The friend who threw the party chose it because she said it was classic and creepy without being gory, like the horror flicks of our goalie-masked generation. I thought she chose it because it was just boring enough to intensify the desire to find something more interesting to do at a coed party. I personally thought it was weird. I've never really thought of birds as scary, except for maybe Big Bird and owls because they do that spinning thing with their heads.

I get it. Hitchcock was going for the subtle scare. Take something little, feathery, and common, something that provides soundtracks for nature walks and golf tournaments, and when you least expect it . . . it bares its bloody beak.

I don't know. I just couldn't see Tweety doing such a thing. I left the party virgin lipped and feather friendly.

Alfred rolled over in his grave. He was brilliantly bizarre, the King of Creepy, and I had the nerve to turn my beak up at him. So for twenty years, he festered in the afterlife, waiting for payback. He patiently waited for me to grow up, finish college, get married, live in a basement apartment for five years, buy and fix up a dumpy townhouse, sell it, buy my first home and live there for several years, sell it, and *finally* build a house out in the country and take up road biking. He wanted me isolated, alone, in a place with lots of open sky and no witnesses. He let me get cozy for a few years, developing bumpkin ways. He watched me smile when I heard the unique honk of sandhill cranes in my back field, followed wild turkey troops down my dirt road, and woke up to the sound of magpies pecking the rain gutters in the middle of the night.

That's right, get cozy, bird lover, Al whispered.

So I was out on my road bike, taking one of my usual loops, pedaling briskly, and enjoying a crisp morning. Hawk sightings are common where I live. They sit all stately and sinister on telephone poles, scouring newly cut fields for unsuspecting mice. I have watched in awe of their cunning grace and speed as they swoop down and rid the world of another pest that could make its way into my pantry.

I didn't think much of the large hawk I noticed perched on a telephone pole ahead of me as I started up the steep hill I make myself ride if I've been chocolate overindulgent. After passing the occupied pole, I heard a swishing noise above me. I looked up just in time to see the hawk dip low over my head then glide up to the next pole. I thought it odd but not aggressive.

I passed the next pole, and moments later, I heard the same swishing. The hawk again swooped in front of my face, a little closer this time. *It could just be coincidence*, I thought, *or not*. I started pedaling slightly faster as the hawk positioned itself on the next telephone pole. As my quads protested my pace, I started thinking about guys I should have kissed in junior high. My legs started to scream. Then I realized it was not my legs screaming; it was a demon creature wildly screeching and coming in for the kill from behind. I turned my head in time to see Alfred Hitch-Hawk dive-bombing like a feathered torpedo toward my head. It was terrifying. Its talons were spread and bearing down like they were ready to give me an Edward Scissorhands makeover. Its beak was open to reveal a freakish wagging tongue, and I felt a sudden empathy for worms everywhere. I answered its scream with my own and commanded my legs to accelerate. I hunkered down into race position to increase aerodynamics, but Hitch-Hawk already had me. My chin hit my chest as the feathered fiend bashed into my head, and I heard scraping noises on my helmet. In shock, I almost lost my balance, but adrenaline kicked in, and I devoured Quad-Killer Hill in record time. As I sped away, I heard an audio montage of a bird screeching and an old man laughing.

When I got home, I took off my helmet to check for evidence. Sure enough, the plastic revealed new grooves. I took it in to show my husband.

"I got attacked by a hawk on my bike today."

"I don't believe you."

"Why not?"

"Because hawks don't attack people, and you have a tendency to exaggerate."

I told him my tale of intimidation and carnage, held out the marred piece of equipment that saved my brain from becoming shredded beef, and explained that literary embellishment for dramatic effect is not exaggeration.

"Fine. I'll bike with you tomorrow. I want to see this 'Hitch-Hawk.'"

As we headed up the hill the next day, we spotted the culprit on the first telephone pole. Its head twitched as we passed, and I prepared for a battle that would confirm my account. The hawk lifted off, spread its wings and gently flew out over the nearby field. We watched as it gracefully bobbed and dipped, making docile patterns in the air. In flight, it did circle over us momentarily before disappearing into a tree. I could feel the smugness emanating from my husband.

"It attacked me!"

"Sure it did."

We biked home in silence. I thought of the spooky silhouette of Alfred Hitchcock they show at the beginning of his movies, his large nose protruding, like a beak. I avoided Hitch-Hawk's territory after that. From the next road over, I could see it hovering, squawking, mocking me.

A few days later, my husband came in from a bike ride. "I believe you."

"What?"

"I believe you got attacked by a hawk." He proceeded to tell me his own Hitch-Hawk encounter. He described a similar attack but said the hawk was even bolder, coming at him head on. He said another smaller hawk came out of the trees and joined in the spree. My husband thought it was probably Hitch-Hawk's mate because there was a large nest up in the trees. I told him there was no need to exaggerate just to make his story better than mine.

Sufficiently spooked, we both avoided the lovebirds' lair. But Alfred was not finished with us yet. A few weeks later, while driving up my street, I noticed a hawk standing in the middle of the road. Feeling that my minivan offered sufficient protection, I proceeded normally. As I came upon it, it didn't fly out of the way as birds usually do. It just sat there, staring at me. At the last minute, I swerved around it, barely missing it. When I checked my "rear window," the hawk stood unmoved and unruffled in the same place, still looking at me. Now neither sky nor land was safe. *Okay, Al, you win. Birds are creepy. Now call off the flock.*

He didn't.

The next day, my husband came in from a bike ride on the same road. "I almost died today."

"I don't believe you."

"Why not?"

"Because I'm the exaggerator, not you."

He then told me the following true story. (Note: Embellishment added for effect.)

While biking downhill toward home, a lone biker noticed a hawk in the middle of the road. He thought it was a little strange because hawks rarely lower themselves to dwell among overlanders. The biker didn't slow down because when there are birds in the road, they usually just fly out of the way. This one did not. Biker and hawk played chicken. The biker came closer. The hawk stood its ground. *Fly out of the way birdbrain!* It didn't. He slammed on his brakes and swerved just as the hawk spread its wings and hopped straight into the wheel spokes. The biker struggled to maintain balance as a puff of feathers swirled around him. He slid through gravel on the road's shoulder, trying to avoid tumbling head first into the ditch below. He managed to pull back onto the road just as the last of the mangled carcass rolled out from the wheel and sprawled out across the road. The shocked murderer pulled to a stop. His heart pounding, his breath short, he looked back at his handiwork. As he contemplated his own brush with death, he thought of the majestic lord of the sky now reduced to a plate of roadkill. On a lone branch above the scene, a songbird whistled an eerie tune.

"You ran down a hawk on your bike?"

"I didn't run it down. It didn't fly out of the way. They're supposed to fly out of the way. They always fly out of the way!"

"Not for us. We're bird cursed. What have you done? Now they'll really have it in for us! You need to go get rid of the evidence. If other birds see what you've done, they'll track us down and attack the house.

They'll eat our dog and our horses in the night. They'll carry off our children."

We found out later from neighbors that an injured hawk had been waddling around on the ground for a few days. Someone had called animal control to come take care of it.

No need. A true kamikaze, it sacrificed its life for the greater good of freaking us out.

"You win, Alfred!" I yelled into the haunted skies. He had sufficiently established the pecking order.

We stayed in more after that. We opted for indoor workouts and prayed for cold weather to prompt an early migration. We cozied up indoors, put in movies, and smooched.

7
The Age of Accountability

FROM THE TIME I WAS a Sunbeam doing jazz hands and spouting "Popcorn Popping" at the top of my irreverent little lungs, I have been taught that the age of accountability is eight years old. By that time, you have hopefully outgrown the worst of childhood mischief, like stuffing your underwear full of dinner mints while your father pays at the restaurant register.

You can still do stuff like that, but at eight years old, your "get out of jail free" card is gone, and you must account for such actions. I never questioned this doctrine until I had an experience one summer that made me wonder.

I know that sounds bold since I'm not a prophet, seer, or revelator. On my best behavior, I probably only weigh in as a mediocre member. I didn't receive this insight through vision; I had this spiritual epiphany during a much more hallowed event—a triathlon.

In case you haven't been bitten by the bug yet, you should know that triathlons are the rage of the middle-aged. When people used to hit midlife, they would do the normal things like bleach their hair or buy an expensive sports car. Those good ol' days are gone. Now, for some reason, you hit thirty- or forty-something and have an uncontrollable urge to pay good money to overexert yourself as you simultaneously master three sport venues while wearing sparse spandex.

One summer, in a freakish fit of overconfidence, I succumbed and did a couple of sprint-length tri's. I was already an avid biker, my daughter coached me through some swim stroke basics, and though I loathe running, I figured I could put one foot in front of the other to complete the 5K. I didn't set any records and avoided drowning, despite the violently thrashing swimmer in front of me, and with my age scrawled in permanent marker on my calf, I crossed the finish line alive.

I admit I was pretty proud of myself. I was also pretty sure I never wanted to train for a tri again. My bike and I are intimate, but I had no desire to step out on it again. I resumed my usual exercise regime and let the leg marking fade into the sunset. For a couple of years afterward, I was perfectly content with my low-end athleticism.

Then one spring a good friend called and said he wouldn't be my friend anymore if I didn't sign up for a tri with him. He knew I had "tried" before, and he knew I didn't have very many friends, so he used this information against me and coerced me into dusting off my tria-tard.

Who knew I was still so susceptible to peer pressure? As I registered online, I could hardly believe the wallet-gauging amount I was paying to engage in organized torture just to keep a friend I now hated more and more with every air-sucking lap.

So why did I decide to "tri" again? First of all, as a tri-virgin, my friend had decided to go for the Olympic length, and I wanted to see him get his padded shorts kicked. (We're really close friends.) Second, most of my days are filled with dishes, laundry, school principal meetings, and so on, and every so often, I feel a need to set down my mop and check my moxie levels.

My training regime was basic—bike two days a week, swim two, run two, working up to full lengths. My friend e-mailed me a high-tech training spreadsheet. Did I mention he is seriously overachiever-ish? I e-mailed back, "Dude, you are into this way more than I am." My goal—finish alive.

At 4:30 a.m. on the day of the tri, my alarm went off, and I immediately decided I could make it through life without friends. But a short time later, we pulled into the parking lot next to a sporty SUV that had the license plate "TRI CHICK" on it. (I warned you; these things are becoming cultlike.) Unfortunately, I left my switchblade at home so I couldn't slash her tires, but I imagined a target on the back of her perky blonde head as she bounded toward registration.

This tri differed from the last one I had done in that the swim was open water in a reservoir. Luckily, I'd had enough smarts to practice an open water swim one time before the actual tri. It's a good thing I did because I discovered something important—I'm afraid of open water swimming.

A week before the tri, I found myself in the middle of a reservoir, floating on my back, mentally trying to find my happy place to stop the hyperventilating. I had no idea how disorienting it was not to be able to see the bottom. Without the pool-lane lines to keep my brain occupied, it started entertaining itself with images of giant catfish latching on to my face or a dead body floating up through the murky abyss.

I tried to block out the trial-run fiasco as I pulled on my rubber suffocation suit and stared out at the official buoy that seemed eons away. I joined the rest of my heat in the water, and when the horn blew, I dove in, hoping the dead body in the water wouldn't be mine.

Halfway to the buoy, I was praying for a giant catfish to come swallow me whole. I somehow managed my way around the lake and breezed through the bike (my fave), but about a mile into the run, I hit the wall.

In moments of great pain, I become the most philosophical. *Why am I doing this? Why are any of us doing this? What is it we are trying to prove?* Through blurry vision, I looked at the ages marked on the calves of those ahead of me and those who were passing me, which were many, and the revelation occurred—the age of accountability is not eight years old. The age of accountability is thirty-seven or forty or fifty-two or whatever age it is that makes you have enough regret about life that you think doing a triathlon will make it all better somehow.

As you swim mind-numbing laps, you think about all the wasted brain space occupied with memorized sitcom dialogues. As your rickety knees jolt with your feet pounding the pavement, you think of landfills full of the empty Hostess boxes you've contributed. When you squish into clothes tighter than someone your age should ever wear in public, you think of the degree you never finished, the business venture that failed, thoughtless words you uttered, failed relationships, unvisited islands, wayward children, deprived childhoods, pesticide toxins, global warming . . . and on and on, etc., etc. And so we swim and bike and run and hope that across that finish line is a sense of accomplishment and empowerment to make peace with what we can't change in the past.

So I crossed the finish line. On the other side of it were my family, some friends, a drink of water, and a cookie.

No regrets.

8
Donkey Talk

I KNOW A TALKING DONKEY is not much of a novelty these days since Eddie Murphy chatted the strange lobes off of Shrek until he gave in and let him be his friend. But in Sunday School one week, I learned that Eddie is no original.

Just when I thought I could get comfortable on the back row and assume my convincing deep-in-spiritual-thought-while-I'm-actually-napping pose, the teacher began with, "Once upon a time—in Old Testament times—a prophet was being a knothead, so the Lord opened the mouth of his trusty donkey to give him a verbal smackdown."

I was astonished. Though I'm no OT scholar, I have read it several times, yet, somehow, I had missed this intriguing true story. Visions, healings, plagues, miracles, yeah, yeah, yeah . . . but talking donkey? There would be no snoozing in Gospel Doctrine class today. I was fully engaged.

The story begins with the prophet Balaam, who is with the children of Israel, who are in hostile takeover mode and are about to wale on Moab. (I'm sure they got the proper permits before staging a battle in a national park.) Balak, King of Moab, saw the trail of blood and carnage left by the Israelites and did not want to give up his view of Delicate Arch. So he dispatched some elders and told them to use the buddy system and go offer Balaam an under-the-table deal to come with them and compromise his people for Balak's victory.

Balaam makes it a matter of prayer, which seems the proper prophet thing to do, though the answer seems like a no-brainer. The scriptures don't say, but I wonder about the wording of that prayer. "Father, can I sell out your chosen and blessed people so I can bask in an establishment job in Balak's kingdom?" Purely hypothetical, of course.

Anyway, Balaam receives a prompt, "Umm, *no*," from the Lord and sends the elders away. Balak sweetens the deal. Not messing around with low-life messengers this time, he sends his princes with superior schmoozing skills and better bling. Balaam shows why he was a prophet with his impressive answer. "If Balak would give me his house full of silver and gold, I cannot go beyond the word of the Lord my God, to do less or more" (Numbers 22:18). However, he shows he is still human and is intrigued by the offer on the table when he says to the princes, "I pray you, tarry ye also here this night, that I may know what the Lord will say unto me more" (Numbers 22:19). Hypothetical once again—"Please, please, please, Father, can I have my cake and eat it too?"

Our Father in Heaven is eternally patient with us and knows about worldly enticement. He gave us the gift of agency so we could choose for ourselves and learn the hard way just how stupid we are sometimes. But when necessary, He's willing to interject a talking donkey into the story to knock some sense into us.

On with the story . . .

Father tells Balaam he can go if he really, really wants to. Balaam skips to the barn and saddles his donkey. He hasn't gone far when, for some reason, he cannot get his donkey to go the way he wants. Balaam, blinded by pride and greed, unknowingly conceded his prophetic seership to his pet donkey, which is now seeing a sword-wielding angel blocking their way. Balaam gets smite happy with a staff, trying to get his donkey to giddyap. The angel holds his ground, and the donkey ends up crushing Balaam's foot against a wall and eventually falling down under Balaam.

Here comes the best part. I will write it verbatim since no ad-libbing could do it justice.

"And Balaam's anger was kindled, and he smote the ass with a staff. And the Lord opened the mouth of the ass, and she said unto Balaam, What have I done unto thee, that thou hast smitten me these three times? And Balaam said unto the ass, Because thou hast mocked me: I would there were a sword in mine hand, for now would I kill thee" (Numbers 22:27–29).

The best part of this dialogue takes place in the space between the donkey asking a question and Balaam answering . . . but wait, *there is no space*. The story in no way indicates that Balaam was the least bit surprised to find that his donkey just opened her mouth and spoke to him. There's no, "In great astonishment, Balaam marveled that his donkey was fluent in Hebrew" or "After coming to, Balaam busted a gut over the fact that his donkey could talk." The exclusion of any signs of surprise or shock on Balaam's part reveals who the donkey really is in this story. Balaam was so wrapped up in getting on his way to undermine his people and receive his honors and riches that a talking donkey didn't even faze him.

I do understand why Balaam didn't see the surreal nature of the situation. I've been like Balaam myself many times—so wrapped up in what I want and think that I find myself talking with or like a donkey and completely missing the angel standing in front of me. It's happened when dealing with a tyrannical toddler or teenager who won't bend to my will. It's happened in Church callings when the people I'm working with don't see things my way. It's happened in my marriage during a martyr tantrum. It's happened with family, friends, neighbors, strangers, and obnoxious drivers. Yes, anger, vanity, and selfishness can be powerful enough to make you miss the fact that you've entered an alternate universe where animals talk.

Well, the story has a happy ending—mostly. Balaam and his donkey make up, and the Lord opens Balaam's eyes so he can see both the angel and his own stupidity. Balaam repents with some serious altar building and does the Lord's will, resulting in a very bad ending for the Moabites.

Balaam and I learned some great lessons. Balaam learned that if he's going to smite his donkey with a staff, he'd better make sure it isn't a magic wand. I learned that if you sleep through Sunday School, you might miss out on awesome learning experiences and talking animals. Balaam and I both learned that the Lord loves us enough that He will go to great lengths to make His point when necessary.

Sometimes I'm tempted to misbehave just to see if the Lord will open the mouth of one of my pets to scold me. My cat Jumpy looks like he might have something profound to say.

9
Talkin' Turkey

THANKSGIVING IS THE TRUE AMERICAN holiday. In the name of gratitude, we glut ourselves on a menu of fats, carbs, starches, proteins, and sugar, then loosen our pants and watch our grotesquely overpaid professional athletes smack each other on the rear and prance around in the glory of their own egos.

My ego, however, takes a serious blow on Thanksgiving. There is an inner sanctum of cooks in my extended kin, and as far as Thanksgiving goes, I have been weighed, measured, and found wanting. I have been the matron of my own household for many years now and have never made the top tier dishes of the Thanksgiving feast.

I have never been allowed to bake the bird, smash the spuds, or defile a perfectly nutritious yam by topping it with s'mores. I've never even made that disgusting creamy bean/almond/canned fried onion–topped casserole thing.

I don't make the cut. I can't make the grade. This seems unfair since I've never actually been invited to prove myself, and as far as I know, an open tryout has never been held.

"Kari, why don't you bring a nice relish tray again. You're so good at that."

Good at a relish tray? I am only worthy of taking vegetables in their raw state and washing and cutting them then serving them with a secret dip recipe entrusted to me by Hidden Valley Ranch.

The most pathetic part is that I actually had to work my way up to relish tray. I used to be assigned half a relish tray. Another relative low on the totem pole and I had to coordinate who would bring carrots and who would bring broccoli. One year we overlapped, and it was bedlam.

Despite the pain of being shut out, I do understand the underlying reasons behind it. Thanksgiving is all about tradition, and the matriarchal women of this family have been cooking and baking their specialty Thanksgiving dishes since before I was a knee-high turkey snitcher.

Aunt Yam covers sweet potatoes with brown sugar and Stay Puft Man droppings then toasts it to perfection. Cousin Cranberry snubs the canned red roll and works gelatin magic with this sour berry that goes virtually forgotten until November. Mother Spud allows nary a lump in her mound of mashed potatoes, and the gravy of turkey drippings is a delicious heart attack in every bite.

And last but certainly not least are the pies—the crown jewels of the Thanksgiving feast. Grandma Crust is the official Grand Dame Pie-maker. Every year she brings the two kinds of pies she has perfected over decades—pumpkin and mincemeat. For desserts made out of orange gourds and shriveled fruit, I'm sure these pies are at their gourmet best. But several hundred years ago, some Spanish monks introduced a delectable evil to the world called "chocolate," and in my opinion, Marie Callender improved upon it when she worked it into pie form.

This is where I initially tried to sneak in—with chocolate pie. One brave Thanksgiving, I made one on the sly. I sneaked it into the car. I smiled all the way over the river and through the woods. I closed my eyes and imagined the family swarming around me, singing praises to me as they shoveled my moussy sensation into their deprived mouths. They would say that I had single-handedly saved Thanksgiving and would name me a family hero and the foremost consultant on Thanksgiving food trends.

After the initial greetings, I slipped back out to the car to get my secret weapon.

"What are you doing?" My husband appeared out of nowhere.

"Uhhhh . . . Just getting something out of the car. What are you doing?" I tried to act casually.

"The same. I saw you come in without the relish tray, so I came back out to get it."

"Oh, aren't you thoughtful." I nervously reached in and pulled out the decoy dish and handed it to him. "Here you go." I closed the back hatch and stood there, trying to wave him away.

"Are you coming in?"

"Yes."

He would't go away. He knows me too well. "What are you up to?"

"Nothing." My mother said I was born with a guilty look on my face.

"Give it up, girl."

I showed him the pie.

"You know you can't take that in there."

I shlumped in defeat. "I know." The pie stayed in the car. I ate it with a plastic fork on the ride home.

The next year, I decided to go with a whisper campaign. I made decadent chocolate peanut butter truffles. While setting the Thanksgiving table, I casually set my sneaky treat next to each glass, like a tantalizing appetizer of good things to come in future Thanksgivings. People liked them—a lot. They told me so in whispered compliments. They all knew I was tampering with the delicate balances of family tradition, and while they savored my tasty token of bravery, they were all afraid for me.

My biggest and most boisterous fan was Grandpa Step. Having married into the family late in life, he was already an outsider and didn't give a flying fig if he bucked tradition. He ate his truffle and anyone else's who was dumb enough to leave chocolate unattended and asked if I had any more stashed in the car. In his ranks, at least, I moved up a few notches that day. We still remain close.

I don't know if it was the truffles or some kind of desperate emergency, but the next year at the last minute, I was asked to make rolls. Rolls! I would actually get to use my oven! I pulled out my melt-in-your-mouth roll recipe and stayed up baking until the wee hours of Thanksgiving morning. I wanted them to be as fresh as possible. I knew I was walking on eggshells, and my offering had to be impeccable if I was ever going to work my way up the ladder. After only a few hours of restless sleep, the phone rang. A muffled voice told me I'd been trumped. A last-minute busybody guest had arrived unexpectedly and insisted on making something for the meal. They told her to make rolls.

After that, the wind blew out of my sails. My ambition went bust. I settled into my proper place and continue to arrange the cast of *Veggie Tales* on a platter every Thanksgiving. Perhaps I'll work up the courage to try to break in again some chilly November Thursday. But for now, I'm giving it up cold turkey.

10
Christmas Fruit Basketcase

FOR A MOM, THERE ARE few surprises at Christmas. My job is to create a season that is meaningful and magical for everyone else. But the magician is not in awe of her own tricks because she knows exactly where the rabbit in the hat came from. It came from PETSMART, aisle 17, for $24.95, hutch and rabbit pellets not included. And guess who will end up cleaning the cage.

One particular year, like most, I was already fully aware of what I was getting for Christmas. My in-laws had called ahead to ask if we would rather have a bucket of wheat or potato flakes for Christmas, and my parents informed me they were doing their shopping at a custodial supply store. (Apparently along with hearing, hips, and eyesight, elfing skills deteriorate with age.) I had helped make the gifts from my younger children at their school parties, and my teenager was saving her precious ducats for an iPod during the after-Christmas sales. (We tipped her off that Santa had already spent his wad on other high-priced electronic devices she wanted.) Due to our current economic status, my husband and I decided to opt out of buying for each other, so any hopes for wrapped magic under the tree for me were dwindling. Not that I expect much; it's just a bit of a growing pain.

Christmas is for children. The magic of childhood is that everything happens for you and around you. Houses and neighborhoods are transformed into illuminated wonderlands. Plates full of goodies arrive at the doorstep. On Christmas morning, things appear that weren't there the night before. Even when you get to help with the baking and decorating, it's not like doing chores; you're an elf in Santa's workshop. You don't know that your help is actually what my grandma calls "fat help" (i.e., help for the sake of the experience, not really help at all, an actual hindering of the project). But it's all part of the magic.

Some of my favorite Christmas memories are actually when I was a big kid, a college kid. You've barely crossed the threshold into adulthood and the belt of real responsibility starts to tighten. After a semester of studying, eating ramen noodles, and scrimping by on part-time wages, I was glad to leave behind roommate drama, jump into my jalopy, and head home for the holidays.

No matter how old you are, when you come home for the holidays, you're a kid again. Mommy is there, wrapping, baking, making her magic, and taking care of everything like always. Little did I know that while I was lying all snug in my bed while visions of sugarplums danced in my head, the ghost of Christmas future lurked outside my door.

I had my season of Christmas magic, and the baton has passed to me. I take it willingly, but a little girl still lingers inside that would like for there to be one thing I didn't buy, make, cook, decorate, arrange, wrap, or plan during Christmas.

Then, I did get a little something—a serious case of PMS.

According to my calculations, I should have been able to pull off my menagerie of Christmas magic well before the "demon days." I was prepared to be the New Year's Nutcracker; I was completely blindsided when I became the Christmas Crackpot.

It was two days before Christmas, and I had just come home from shopping. I came into the room where my husband was sitting, and like a sweet St. Nick, he motioned for me to come sit on his lap. Forgetting the way I'd been eating since Thanksgiving, I plopped down. He attempted to muffle a grunt and then jovially asked, "So, little girl, what do you want for Christmas?" Out of nowhere, it was like I was mourning the loss of my entire childhood in that moment. I started bawling, and a pathetic monologue erupted from my Scroogy soul.

"Where's my magic? Who's my Santa? Why is it that a big, fat, happy *man* gets all the credit for Christmas? It's probably because Mrs. Claus is in a coma by Christmas Eve after getting everything ready. Where's my crew of jolly elves to help out? You know what's under the tree for me this year? A pile of wrapping paper to throw out. A batch of dishes from the fancy meal the night before. The pile of bills to be paid for all the stuff I just bought that will be broken, lost, or boring before New Year's. Decorations to be put away, kids to keep busy for another week, and eight pounds of cellulite on my thighs. That's what's under the tree for me. I know you're getting ripped off this year too, but at least the gifts the kids open will be a surprise for you. Then you get to escape back to work the day after, and I'm stuck sweeping up the elf dust."

I was like Sally in the Great Pumpkin patch, bellowing out the wretched pangs of holiday disappointment. I sat there sobbing while my poor husband patted my back and wished he really were Santa Claus, the department store kind who could hand the bawling kid back to her mommy. But I was the mommy, so there was no one to hand me off to, except the men in the white coats, which I think my husband was seriously considering.

After a few minutes and a few quarts of saline water, I regained some composure. (The good thing about mood swings is the swing part.) I slithered off my husband's dilapidated lap, wiped away my tears and the mascara remnants, and apologized for the outburst.

My poor husband made an attempt. "I'll go buy you something if you want."

Embarrassed, I replied, "No, it's okay. I'm sorry. I don't know where that came from."

We exchanged forced smiles, both knowing exactly where that came from. I shuffled out of the room to go find an undiscovered hiding place for the gifts I'd just bought to keep the magic facade in tact.

Two days later, Christmas came and was full of magic. There was even a little magic under the tree for me. My husband had broken our agreement (prompted by my episode, no doubt) and bought me a beautiful nativity. As I touched the smooth figure of Mary, I thought of this selfless mother who humbly and quietly provided the world with true Christmas magic. I recognized that it was an honor to carry on the motherly tradition of providing Christmas magic for those I love. Non-hormone-prompted tears fell from my eyes as I looked over at my Santa Claus, a magician in his own right.

I don't resent that Santa Claus gets top billing at Christmas. I know Mrs. Claus is the cog behind the wheels, but it's good business to have the more emotionally stable partner act as spokesperson. And I bet they make allowances on Christmas Day and serve Mrs. Claus some cookies and milk in her padded cell.

11
Easter Someday

I LIKE THE EASTER BUNNY. I love the concept of celebrating the coming of spring with a possibly humongous rabbit that hides eggs, fills baskets with candy, and strongly suggests you buy new Sunday clothes.

It's fun. It's funny, and I like eggs, candy, and new clothes. My pleasure in the Easter Bunny in no way diminishes the reverence and awe I feel for what Easter really celebrates. It's probably a sin to like the Easter Bunny, and this, combined with my catalog of much deadlier sins, makes me truly thankful for my Savior Jesus Christ and the price He paid for me.

There are those who properly separate church and state and do the heathen bunny stuff on Saturday and save Sunday for the religious focus. Some have banned the bunny altogether. They're probably right, even if I do hate them for it. (I already admitted to being a sinner.) I dare to think a little springtime frivolity and proper sacred observance can be combined tastefully. I don't know why I always think such stupid things.

One Easter morning, I arose early enough—I thought—to enjoy a little bunny booty with the kids and still be ready for church on time. We found the elusive eggs and then ate them for breakfast with a side of Peeps. After what I felt was sufficient silliness, I ushered the kids off to wash and put on their non-new Sunday best—an abundance of April snow showers that year having dampened my spring shopping spirit. (My husband probably prayed for it.)

Then the phone rang. It was the devil calling to inform me that he'd won my soul. Actually, it was our choir director calling to tell me my oldest daughter and I were supposed to be at the church in fifteen minutes to practice for the Easter program. I semi-yelled downstairs to inform the kids of our new deadline. I told them to skip baths, do hygiene basics, and meet me in the car ASAP. I hoped our transgression of semi-shabby appearance would be offset by our offering of Easter program participation.

I did a speed-dial Sunday look on myself and met my daughter on the way out to the car, thinking we were actually going to make it. We would observe this sacred day properly, dang it!

Just then, my other two children walked in the back door in their pajamas covered in mud and hay. They had not gone to get ready when I had told them to. They weren't downstairs to hear my change-of-plans announcement. Instead, they had gone out to the barn on this Easter Sunday to play with their pet bunny. Yes, we had a real bunny. An animal that had gone completely ignored and neglected since our unfortunate and accidental acquisition of him eight months prior. An animal that I had secretly let out of its cage twice to run away and hopefully be found by a nearby wolf but instead ended up in our annoyed neighbor's yard. Yet, on this Easter Sabbath, my children's interest in bunnies was piqued, and they remembered that we had one, so they hippity-hopped on the bunny trail out to visit our Peter Cottontail.

The devil laughed. There was a price to be paid for my Easter Bunny–loving ways.

What happened next is far from Easter-ish. There was some yelling, screaming, blaming, and frantic spit-bathing. I sent my husband and daughter ahead since they were ready and could at least save their souls. I missed the practice but managed to arrive on time for sacrament meeting with the two rabbit renegades. We hurried in and sat down in a pew behind my beautiful, thin friend who has nine children, who were all dressed in sharp new suits and pastel dresses with not a speck of hay in their curled and combed hair.

I then celebrated Easter properly. I sat in my pew, bowed my head, and cried. I cried and prayed for forgiveness for screaming at my kids, for eating Peeps for breakfast, for liking chocolate and bunnies (except for the one I own and tried to kill), for trying to kill my bunny, and for not having nine children—or even three clean ones. In that moment, I was both extremely sad and grateful that the only perfect Being to ever walk the earth had died and risen for such a pathetic collection of sins. I know He did, which is what Easter is all about.

The holiday did improve, except for a speaker who went off on a tangent about estrogen levels from the pulpit, then I broke the Sabbath only slightly further by tidying up the house for the arrival of grandparents for dinner. The sun even made a showing after days of dismal weather.

It wasn't the perfect Easter Sunday, but in the end, it turned out well. I hope eventually my boorish ways will refine and I'll be able to celebrate Easter properly. In the mean time, I'll try to reconcile my relationship with the bunny.

12
The Mother of All Holidays

WHOEVER DECIDED MOTHER'S DAY SHOULD be on Sunday was not LDS. This is the one day a week when every family member has to be cleaned and dressed up better than usual and arrive somewhere all at the same time—preferably on time and prepared to fulfill whatever collective callings/responsibilities you have for Church that day. While other mothers are perusing around a chocolate fondue fountain at the local bistro's Mother's Day brunch buffet and using their gift cards to break the Sabbath at the mall, we're slapping Sunbeams around while a raw roast sits in the Crock-Pot we forgot to turn on back home.

The sacrament meeting Mother's Day program is meant to be a golden tribute to motherhood through word and song. Generous and touching quotes, stories, and examples pour from the souls of appreciative children and husbands. But everyone knows LDS women are major guilt mongers. Every gushing, complimentary word offered only makes us ruthlessly compare ourselves to idealized expectations and torment ourselves for everything we did or didn't do in our mothering. When the darling little Primary kids stand at the front and sing a medley of "Mother Dear" and "I Often Go Walking," all we notice is our own kid's bad case of bedhead and the inside of his nostrils from the face he is pulling.

Every once in a while, there is a talk given that makes us all feel better, well almost all of us. One lovely May day, a young man paid homage to his mother's sacrifice of giving him life with a dazzling description of his emergency C-section birth, where he "got ripped from his mother's belly like gutting a fish." He then acknowledged his mother's efforts to fulfill her many responsibilities by putting his own spin on a well-known saying, "My mother is always running around like a head with its chicken cut off."

I'm sure this fine young man meant the fish guts and missing chicken references to be a gift of appreciation for his mother. He probably looked down at her in the congregation and felt all proud when he saw he had brought tears to her eyes. We all cried with her in solidarity then went home and laughed our fish guts out.

So on that special holiday each year, I offer a heartfelt "Happy Mother's Day" to moms everywhere. Here's hoping you don't come home to a cold roast, that your chicken remains securely adhered to your head, and that you don't feel like a gutted fish.

13
Kari, Larry, and Lilacs

"MIRROR, MIRROR ON THE WALL, I am my mother after all."

I gave my mom a magnet with this saying on it for Mother's Day one year. It's probably the best gift I've ever given her because out of all her children, I'm pretty sure I said, "I'm never going to do that when I'm a mom" the most, which, of course, came back to bite me big time. She deserves an "I told you so" moment with me.

However, what's really freaking me out is how much I'm becoming like my dad. It seems only natural that my mothering would resemble my own mother's, but I hardly expected to eat humble pie paternally as well. My dad's name is Larry, and my suspiciously similar name of Kari was his idea, which I now see as part of a grand scheme to curse me on both counts.

One of these "Lar' moments," as my husband has labeled these genetically motivated mishaps that eerily resemble my father's behavior, occurred as I found myself pulled off to the side of the road on a sunny Monday in May with a bucket of water in one hand and a knife in the other. I was standing in front of a lilac bush. I don't know whose lilac bush it was, and that's how it should be because it's all part of a long-established family tradition—swipe lilacs to decorate graves for Memorial Day.

Memorial Day is a holiday that celebrates and honors family heritage, so I guess it's fitting that I should do as my forefather did— check to make sure no one is looking before mugging a stranger's bush.

I remember year after year hunkering down into the sticky Naugahyde seat of our big yellow station wagon as my father performed the dirty deed. I wondered why we couldn't just go to the store and buy mums like a normal family. My mother voicing this and other exasperated questions about my father's behavior while ducking below the dashboard was all part of this grand tradition. But my father's explanation was staunch and sentimental: "Mom and Grandma like lilacs."

I don't know for sure, but I have my own theory as to why lilac lovers run in my family. My paternal grandmother and her mother before her farmed, ranched, and raised large families in one of the most inhospitable regions in the country. Randolph, Utah, is a forgotten settlement of only a few hundred residents, yet this Western sink often receives the honor of being the coldest place in the country on national weather reports. As my grandpa used to say, "There are only two seasons here: winter and July."

As lingering winter weather would commandeer weeks that should show signs of spring, I imagine these hardy women watched longingly out the window at the lilac bush on the property, waiting for a sign from this spring bloomer that Old Man Winter was releasing his grip.

Lilacs represented a coming season of liberation. The kids would take their noise outside. The stove would need less wood. Laundry could be hung outside to dry instead of being strewn all over the house. Fresh produce from the garden would replace bottled goods. The barn thermometer would read above zero for the 4:00 a.m. milking. Yes, lilacs were lovely on many levels. My father wanted to honor that, and nothing, not even No Trespassing and Beware of Dog signs were going to keep him from doing so.

I did my share of whining when my parents loaded us up and drove us to the cemeteries of Yawnville on Memorial Day. But my parents win again because now I recognize it's important to know where you came from. How else will you know whom to blame for your health issues, figure and facial misfortunes, and annoying personality traits?

Memorial Day offers the opportunity to unplug from the present and pay homage to your past. An older neighbor once told me about how on Memorial Day in his community growing up, he had to put on a suit and tie to go to the cemetery. Everyone wore their Sunday best for a program that included a flag ceremony and memoir readings. Afterward, there was lots of visiting about family and the good ol' days. I certainly prefer sporting a hoodie and jeans to chiffon and heels when roving the cemetery, but I do think modern generations are becoming too casual about honoring their heritage for Memorial Day.

For some people, it is the day for pulling the boat out of winter storage for a season-christening spin on the frigid reservoir. Perhaps their ancestors came over on the Mayflower, and jumping the wake on a boogie board helps them feel akin to them. Campgrounds fill up with luxury RVs so people can spend the extended weekend eating microwave popcorn and watching satellite TV from their pop-out couch in the great outdoors. It's a serious stretch, but I suppose you could count it as a form of "circling the wagons" like the pioneers did when they crossed the plains.

As for my family and me, we will carry on the tradition of making the pilgrimage to the hollers of our heritage on Memorial Day. My father will be pleased to know that along with black-market blooms, the whining tradition is also well represented by his grandchildren now. For pure torment, like my parents did, I bore them on the way there with my own stories that start with "When I was a kid . . ." They gasp in disbelief when I tell them we only had five TV channels and we had to actually get up off the couch and turn a circular thing called a "dial" to change the channel. But over time, my family stories and memories marinated and refined into respect and reverence for my ancestry, and it is my hope that my efforts will eventually have the same effect on my offspring.

From war heroes to witches, from Mormon Apostles to moon-shiners, our family's got it all, baby, and what better way to spend a day than gettin' jiggy with the ghosts of relations past? I stand next to my progenitors' gravestones and tell my children, "Once upon a time, in a village far, far away from civilization, three brothers married three sisters." It's important to know that the abnormalities they reveal in therapy later in life are not directly my fault.

Then, in completion of the Memorial Day "Lar' moment," I place the stolen lilacs on my grandmother's and great-grandmother's graves. I tell my children about how my grandmother lost her mother at age eleven and had to help raise her younger siblings. No wonder she assumed her mother's favorite flower. The precious lilac blooming season is beautiful, fragrant, and brief, like her mother's life.

Maybe it's not such a bad thing to inherit a few traits from your parents. I anxiously await the day when one of my daughters catches herself tap dancing next to the baggage claim carousel at a crowded airport while her kids wander away, pretending not to know her, and thinks, "I just had a Kar' moment!"

14
Testimony and Tuna Fish

LIFE LESSONS OFTEN COME IN odd ways, which is my personal preference. While I was serving as the ward Primary chorister, a learning experience spontaneously came full circle during a Singing Time presentation. I was midproduction and in need of some chalk. I quickly ventured over to look for some in the cabinet under the Primary pulpit. I scoured the cabinet contents—pencils, paper, thumbtacks, crayons . . . can of albacore tuna? Even with the Church's emphasis on food storage, a single can of tuna under the pulpit truly is a fish out of water.

Forgetting that forty people were in the room waiting for me to produce chalk and continue, I started laughing. I quickly caught myself and resumed. The mostly juvenile congregation seemed unfazed by my little outburst, since I'd had this calling about a year and they'd grown accustomed to Sister Rich's little oddities.

I don't know why the can of tuna was there. Maybe someone was teaching about the loaves and fishes and, like the miracle itself, there was enough and to spare. Maybe someone was taking their food storage very seriously and toted spare canned goods in their church bag and one escaped. Whatever the reason for the can of tuna, it made me laugh because it provided a perfect irony of a dilemma that had been vexing me at the time.

As members of The Church of Jesus Christ of Latter-day Saints, we strive for perfection but are far from perfect. We are sinners labeled as Saints because together we are doing a great work despite our mortal imperfections. While many wonderful, even miraculous, things happen in the Church, there is plenty that goes on that is, well, a little fishy.

We all have different backgrounds, understandings, personalities, and quirks that we bring to the organization. We are taught, trained, and counseled about how to run the kingdom, but as we serve and follow one another in a church of lay ministry, sometimes there is resemblance to the court jester act.

I admit, sometimes church is difficult. We've all sat through testimony meetings of travelogues, thankful-monies, family situation TMI, and anatomically incorrect health reports. (My personal favorite is a misspoken use of *scrotum* for *sternum*.) We've endured sacrament meeting talk chastisements and unauthorized calls to repentance, discussions on local water rights, and Three Nephite sightings. Parents don't even want to know what children raise their hands and reveal boisterously in Primary, and Relief Society's "60 Seconds of Good News"—let's not even go there.

Of course, things won't always go status quo, even in the true Church, because we are mere mortals. But when I attend my meetings and activities and serve in callings, I do hope for at least some soul enlightenment. It's hard when I go to church needing my cup refilled and I return home even more parched than before because of the oddities that occur. They can cause distraction from the Spirit, like finding a can of tuna in the Primary pulpit. And at the time I found the tuna, it seemed like there had recently been an overage of albacore antics going on at church, and I was struggling.

Lest anyone reach for the protruding beam in my eye, I freely acknowledge personal guilt. In my own spiritual journey, I have certainly dumped my share of dreck into the pit, which was part of the issue. I wondered how often I had been the camel hogging the watering hole when someone had come to drink from living waters. I worried if any of us got anything meaningful out of these religious rituals when we were all taking turns spiritually spewing.

Then it happened—some wonderful, insightful experiences answered my questions, despite my unworthiness to receive them. I was listening to a general conference talk by President Henry B. Eyring. He spoke about the Savior's ministry and how He spent His time among sinners, lunatics, those possessed by evil spirits, people who were sick physically/mentally/emotionally/spiritually. I realized this description could easily describe any congregation in the modern Church at any given time, and each of us has probably been in any or all of these states at one time or another.

We're all there, just like in the Savior's era—a time-warp truckload of rubber-roomies relishing in the company of the promised Savior because we know He has what we need. He loved them, and He loves us, even in our dysfunction. There is something to gain in our religious practice, even when it turns a little looney-palooza at times.

I was blessed with two other experiences to emphasize the point. (Due to the fact that I'm spiritually dense, Heavenly Father has to use remedial techniques with me.) I was reading the *Doctrine and Covenants Children's Reader* with my son, and we just happened to be on the story of the night the prophet Joseph Smith was dragged from his home by a mob to be beaten, poisoned, tarred and feathered, and left for dead. His family and friends cared for him through the night. The next morning, he presided and spoke to a congregation that included members of the mob. When we finished reading the story, my son asked me why I was crying.

I had been humbled. No matter what happened the night before, no matter who was going to be at church in the morning, Joseph would attend to his Church responsibilities, humbly serving God and His children.

The finale came from the Book of Mormon. (I marvel when, in my personal scripture study, I just happen to be on a chapter that offers answers to a current concern.) I was reading the writings of Mormon, who was called at a very young age to lead a band of wicked people into a series of fruitless battles. At one point, he was so frustrated he refused to take part anymore (completely relatable). He later repented of his refusal and returned to be their leader. Mormon didn't return to help his people because they or their cause had changed for the better. In fact, they had become even more wicked than before. Mormon served them for the change that would take place in himself. He exercised faith in what he didn't yet understand, believing in God's promises for him in the end.

There is going to be the occasional "can of tuna" that randomly pops up. Prophets and even the Savior Himself had to learn to work with and around them. My responsibility is to look beyond the fishiness with faith. These three experiences reminded me that the people I serve and the situation in which I serve are just a means to an end. How I become more Christlike as I serve is what matters. I had been spiritually fed a three-course meal, with a side of tuna.

15
To DI For

I love Disneyland. I think it is perfectly justified in calling itself "the happiest place on earth." It's clean and themed from the tip of Sleeping Beauty's castle to the pinafore-clad bathroom towel attendant.

But I visited a magical place that I think deserves the title "the slap-happiest place on earth"—Deseret Industries. Better known by its jiggy name of DI, this place is the LDS community's best kept secret. There are other second-hand stores—the Salvation Army, Savers—and I don't mean to slight these fine establishments I have patronized myself. But browsing through the residue of Mormon culture holds a mystique all its own.

I went in one day in a busy huff and rush to find a costume for a disco skit my son would be involved in. I knew I could probably find something online, but that would require shipping, bidding, or some other cyber-involvement I wasn't up for. So I headed to the place I knew could make all my retro wishes come true.

Though I frequently make donation drop-offs, it had been a while since I'd shopped the DI. Not that I'm a snob. My closet and household contain many timeless treasures acquired from the hallowed halls of this second-hand sanctuary. My babies wore many DI specials when even blue light specials were beyond our budget.

Before we could ever afford Disneyland, my young children thought the DI was an amusement park because we took frequent field trips there for pure entertainment. My kids would jump on rusty mini tramps, ride flat-tire trikes around the back lot, hug cycloped teddy bears, rummage through bins of naked Barbies, and clomp around the aisles in moon boots. They'd each choose a toy, a forgotten VHS blockbuster, and a "sparkly" from the jewelry bin, and head home having only spent a few bucks.

As my kids have gotten older and life has gotten busier, my DI-ing has diminished, but all the magical memories came flooding back as I walked through the double doors.

I was a little worried I wouldn't be able to find an outfit from the 70s for my son, since it seems like such a long time ago that I graced the earth with my presence during that groovy decade. I was sure the 90s were well represented and thought even the 80s were slowly making their way out of people's closets. But I speculated the 100 percent polyester-clad 70s were probably defying decomposition in landfills by now. I needn't have worried. The DI does not disappoint.

As I perused racks, I found polyester lavender bell bottoms and a gold and brown striped shirt with a collar so large that a dainty breeze would make the occupant airborn. I saw dresses straight from Marsha Brady's closet, platform boots that would make Donny Osmond reach the top shelf again, and plaid slacks that probably fit some cool cat tight enough to give an anatomy lesson. Yes, the 70s were alive and well at the DI—as well as any other era you might want to visit. I looked around and laughed out loud. I loved this place! It was hilarious, nostalgic, and frightening all at the same time. To think that such items had only recently been purged from the households of my community was both disturbing and delightful.

I had walked into this store with the intent to hurry, find, buy, and get back to my to-do list, but I suddenly found myself unable to leave. The three bulging racks of tacky Hawaiian shirts alone would entertain me for hours. They whispered tales of uber-conservative retired Mormon couples, who, after raising eight kids on teachers' salaries, were finally taking a dream vacation to Hawaii. In hang-loose splendor, they put on shorts, drank virgin Mai Tais, and bought shirts with patterns and colors resembling scenes from "Pink Elephants on Parade." Oh, the stories this place could tell! I was running behind schedule, but there were still so many departments to explore!

I became giddy as I ran to the "As Is" section. What a great name. Come shop through other people's discarded junk that is so random and useless it could only be categorized by "As Is"! There I found the homemaking craft graveyard, where many toll painting mishaps and glue gun gone-wrongs are laid to rest. There are racks of novice inventor contraptions, Chia Pets minus chia, and disturbing artistic expressions.

The sleepwear department is a riot. The number of full-length housecoats made of fabric chainmail and industrial zippers to the chin made me wonder how we'd managed to multiply and replenish the earth. WARNING: There is a lingerie rack. I proceeded cautiously because the thought of used lingerie repulsed me. When I told my husband of my loathing, he said, "What do you mean? It's probably the least-used stuff in the whole place."

The furniture department is RC Willey-Nilly. The contrasting rows of well-loved La-Z-Boys and brand new Health Riders would probably make Brigham Young rethink naming us after a word that means "industry." I plunked down on a couch upholstered with stains and smells and almost sank to the floor. I listened closely to see if I could actually hear the voice of Andy Williams coming from the velvet-covered speakers of the furniture console stereo in front of me. The old man walking past must have thought he heard it too because he sat down next to me, closed his eyes, and smiled. The presence of my impromptu companion awakened my awareness to the crown jewels of the DI: the Peeps.

I glanced around the room. I could hardly go to Times Square to find such a human sampling. There were obvious day-trippers like me—those who had come for something specific. Somehow they had managed to stay focused and on task, poor folks. There were bargain hunters, apathetic wanderers, people watchers, and field trip moms (nostalgic pang). Like in any good grotto, loiterers, idlers, and skulkers were all well represented. But the DI has an exclusive population not even Central Park can boast of: the True D-Ite.

Looking over my shoulder, I discovered a clan of them occupying half a row of recliners. There were five of them, and the first lady in the line had a bin of jewelry in her lap. She picked up each piece and molested it with her eye before handing it down the line, each person following suit. The final inspector worked a Dora the Explorer magnifying glass over it then assigned each piece to one of two piles: keepers and duds. I had happened upon the lair of a D-Ite pirate mob searching for hidden treasure. You could see in the eyes of a Captain Jack among them that he was dreaming of a celebrity appearance on *Antiques Roadshow*.

This horde perfectly represents the D-Ite: the Stock Stalker. There is definitely hidden treasure to be found at the DI. Sometimes people don't know the value of what they are throwing out, and the D-Ites are ready to prey upon their carelessness. A friend of mine once found an old Book of Mormon with notes and mission letters from Parley P. Pratt in it. But the casual caller rarely makes such a find. To hit the jackpot, you have to enter a whole other DI dimension. You have to be ready for a committed relationship. You have to follow restocking schedules, team up with other DI dwellers, and make a new groove in an old La-Z-Boy cushion. You have to frequent "As Is" unafraid. But one day, who knows? You might just find a full set of Charlie's Angels glass tumblers intact!

Though I was a Johnny-Come-Lately, I wanted to go home with a prize. I was anxious to find a shortcut into the DI down-low. The pirate clan looked exclusive, so I ditched my couchmate and scanned for someone who looked connected to hook me up. I noticed a couple of workers huddled in the children's apparel department, sharing a guffaw over something. The staff. Of course. Make honey with the worker bees, and you're in, baby. I ventured over in hopes of closing in on a golden nugget. One worker was holding up a graphic T-shirt. "They put the funniest things on shirts these days," he said between laughs. The other could hardly respond between chortles. "I know. They're so clever." I couldn't stand it. I sidled up behind them for a sticky beak. On a ratty, neon yellow T-shirt was a picture of a fork talking to a plate via conversation balloon that said, "The cheese said it was OK." I guess you had to be there.

Since Siskel & Ebert were no help, I decided to brave the back lot alone. I was on my wiley way and thick into my mission when, suddenly, the inevitable happened . . . My cell phone rang. The caller ID listed "home." Like the demon coin in *Somewhere in Time*, it brought me back to my century and reality. Duty called, and I answered it.

"Did you get my costume, Mom?"

"Yeah, bud, I got it."

"When are you coming home? When's dinner? I'm starving."

Game over. My golden ticket had expired, and it was time to wave good-bye to the Oompa-Loompas and leave Candyland. I made my purchase and headed home. But I had scored more than a groovy get-up. I had found a prize. This eclectic, quirky place had taken me on a serendipitous adventure and refilled my cup. I was ready to return to tending to the needs of my family, household, and life. I was ready to go home and use it up, wear it out, make it do, then donate it to the DI.

16
My Slopes and Dreams

"How irresponsible do you feel today?"

My heart skipped. It was *his* voice flirting over the phone. The tenor cooing of my first college crush. I was not in high school anymore. This was a man. He was in his twenties, was able to produce a five o'clock shadow, and had student loans and everything.

"I'm feeling fairly irresponsible. Why do you ask?" I was pulling on my snow boots to make the uphill trek against canyon winds to 7:30 a.m. Math 105. It would take very little to coerce me.

"Well, a new layer of powder fell in the night, and I think the slopes are calling our names. Are you in?"

Was he asking me out? His verbiage sounded more one-of-the-gang-ish than Emily Post courting, but he hadn't mentioned that any other members of his harem or posse had been included. I pictured him in snow pants, a sporty parka, and shades and decided, gang or not, I was in.

"You know, I was just thinking I heard the call of the wild myself this morning." My second semester of college, and I was already playing hooky for a guy, but I had a very repressed high school dating career, so I had some wild oats to sow. I imagined myself crawling out of my dorm window and hopping on the back of his motorcycle with my skis.

"Great. It's a date, then." He said it. It *was* a date! We were off to Winter Wonderland. Maybe later on we'd conspire as we dreamed by the fire.

Then he said, "Say, do you still have some of those passes to Powder Mountain left?"

Snow globe scene shattered. He was only after one thing. He wanted me for my pass. In one of our many platonic conversations, I must have mentioned that I had some ski passes I had earned working at a ski resort in the fall. Why buy the cow when you can ski for free?

"Yea, I think I have one . . . or two left." My mind reconfigured his image—snow pants sagging in the rear and frost hanging from his nose hairs. "Should I pack myself a lunch?" As this date had turned Dutch, I didn't want to assume anything.

"Hey, don't worry about that. I'll slap a couple of sandwiches together for us. It's the least I could do since you're taking me skiing!" The theme from *Thoroughly Modern Millie* played in my head.

"Make mine baloney." I was sure he had enough for the both of us.

No, it wasn't a match made on heavenly slopes that day, but the skiing was killer. It wasn't a completely wasted pass since he drove, brought lunch, and pretended to believe my lie that I couldn't do moguls because I had hereditary bad knees.

This frozen episode from my powdery past played through my head as I lay on my back in the snow next to my son near the bunny hill lift.

"Are you ready to go yet, bud?"

"Not yet. I'm still tired."

Yeah, I shouldn't push him. We'd already gone down the hill twice. I shouldn't be such a tyrant. My brain calculated the per-run cost of his pass as my retinas burned from staring into the winter sun. I was trying to be patient. Wasatch Mountain winters hold many magical memories for this Utah girl, and though I love to ski now, the learning process of my childhood reels as a montage of chilling torture scenes.

It was at that very resort that I skied for the first time at age twelve. My dad brought us up for a "five bucks after five" deal with some family friends and borrowed equipment. The friends were five brothers, who were older than we were and avid skiers. My father, King Con, pawned his four daughters off with the boys for free ski lessons. He preached some convoluted doctrine about peer instruction being the most effective way to learn and slalomed away with the boys' father. What followed was far from the barn-raising ballet in *Seven Brides for Seven Brothers*. The Pontipee brothers were easy on the eyes, good teachers, and very gracious under the circumstances. The poor guys had come under false pretenses of a night of black diamond hot-doggin' and had ended up as ski nannies.

I remember spending more time in the snow fighting with my ill-fitting equipment than actually skiing. I thought the lift was an evil monster designed to make a tween girl who could moonwalk like a *Thriller* video dancer look like a complete clodhopper in front of her foxy peer instructor. By the end of the night, I was a preteen popsicle and was pretty sure I never wanted to ski again.

As I looked over at my son's frozen stare, purple lips, and limp appendages sprawled across the snow, I figured his skiing sentiments were the same. This wasn't our first time skiing. For three seasons, I had slaved to light the Winter Olympic torch under my kids' uninterested bodies. Unlike my dad, gullible friends and ski lesson were beyond my budget, so I had to beat a love of skiing into my kids myself. My girls were enduring the learning process well enough, but my son continued to buck the system.

How did my dad do it? How did he get me back into bindings after such a rough premier? I don't recall the follow-up outings being any better. I remember being jerked out of a sound sleep at 6:00 a.m. on frosty Saturday mornings and hearing Dad mutter that the ski day would be half gone if I didn't get a move on.

I remember bracing myself in wide snowplow stance against blinding blizzards, hoping the trail I was on eventually led to a lift. I remember glancing longingly up at the warm, happy people in the window of the lodge restaurant, eating burgers and fries, while I sat on our tailgate attempting to sink chattering teeth into frozen PB&J. I remember falling, flailing, fumbling, and frequently checking the time to see how much longer until I could go home. What had made me do it?

Not only was the learning process rough, but we also earned our passes the hard way. My father was no sugar daddy, so the only way my middle-class family was able to ski was working at a ski resort in the fall clearing the slopes of overgrowth—a handshake deal Dad had finagled with the owner to shmooze his family into a recreational sport more common among the high-society set because of its steep price tag. We spent hours scaling black diamond slopes, hacking at weeds and clipping quakies, to earn our days of frozen torment. How did the mad genius pull it off? How did he get his gaggle of geese to submit the precious weekends of our youth to his will? I tried to think.

First, my dad possesses an intensity that has unexplainable hypnotic powers. Second, he was master of making a situation more painful should you dare to choose contrary to his wishes. "Sure, you can stay home today. I'll leave a list of things you'll need to get done while we're gone."

I had done enough of those lists to know that freezing my buns off was the more pleasant choice. So time after miserable time I cowered and endured and categorized Warren Miller as a psycho. But, somewhere, somehow, in a flurry of frigid experiences, something amazing happened—I learned to ski and learned to love to ski. One of my favorite authors, Richard Peck, once said, "Reading is a discipline before it is a pleasure." My dad knew the same was true of skiing. He knew if he could just get us to go up on those slopes and gut it out, eventually the frostbite would heal and the fun would begin. And begin it did.

There was the first time I braved a small jump and landed it with my friends cheering me on. There were the lift rides with my sisters, laughing and talking while keeping a keen eye below for mock-worthy biffs. Taking trails through the trees to follow a tall, shy redhead who had a wicked quick wit if you got close enough to hear him. I got close enough.

Moody night skiing under the stars, sunny spring skiing speeding down the slopes in a T-shirt, jeans, and sunglasses, wishing the day would last forever. The Pontipees became like brothers, and having ski skills hooked me up with other friends with access to condos at ski resorts, where we spent luxurious weekends skiing and hot-tubbin'.

Guys who ski dig girls who ski, which resulted in super slope dates, where sometimes the guys even paid for my pass and lunch inside the lodge. As a newlywed, I introduced my husband to skiing and took great pleasure in watching my prince charming fall off his snowy white horse. My coming of age story had unfolded on the slopes, and I just wanted to offer my son the opportunity to collect his own mountain mementos.

So there I was playing snow slug, wishing I had been blessed with my father's hypnotic gifts. I tried to think up a poisonous work list if he didn't get off his keister soon, but I gave up and sat up.

"I'm going to ski, dude. I'll go take a couple of runs and come back for you, okay?"

He sat up and scowled at the lift that had kicked him off during our attempts to get on and off. "Okay, Mom. I'll just be here."

My heart ached as I got up and put my skis on. I knew plenty of kids who grew up ski-free in Utah and turned out all right—mostly.

Then the ski gods smiled down upon us. A puffy, pink-decked ski bunny, who was probably a year or two younger than my son, confidently swished past us into the lift line. All by herself, she lined up with the chair and let it scoop her up. My son looked on.

"Well, I'm off to the slopes. I'll be back." I skied away.

After a couple of exhilarating solo runs, I came back to find the snow bank where I'd left my son empty. I looked around. Then I heard an excited yell from the lift, "Hey, Mom! Up here!" There he was, grinning ear-to-ear and waving excitedly from a lift chair, not far behind the pink snow bunny. "I got on and off by myself and already went down the hill once."

The next generation of ski bum was born. He didn't need hypnosis or a list, just some space and a little lesson from Mother Nature about the birds and the bees . . . and bunnies.

"Right on, dude. I'm right behind you."

A mountain full of memories awaits.

17
Arithmaticked

WE ARE NOT MATH PEOPLE. Our family would definitely be categorized as right-brainers and probably flatter ourselves at that since no-brainers is probably the most accurate classification. We are a clan of artists and writers, and when the world goes to pot, which is probably sooner than later, we will meld into nomadic vagrancy all too easily, I'm afraid. So the fact that my teenager achieved straight As and a D+ in geometry is not entirely her fault, though we didn't tell her that.

We pumped her full of hyped-up parenting jargon, like, "You can do anything you set your mind to," and "Visualize yourself getting an A, and take the steps to make it a reality." But in the end, phrases like, "Bring that math grade up or your life will become bereft of social interaction with any human form," seemed to be the most effective. She gave us the usual excuses: "I really do try hard. I just don't get it." She even resorted to the ultimate cop-out: "It's not my fault. The teacher doesn't explain it at all, and then she won't even help us." Despite the genetic strikes against her and the claim of substandard instruction, we didn't buy it that her best efforts would only produce a D+. Tough love, baby.

I remember hating math, sitting in class watching my middle-aged teacher work his greasy comb-over with one hand while using the other to write useless gibberish on the board. My interest only piqued when I heard the word *pie*. While I sat daydreaming about my future as the lead singer of an all-girls rock band, I thought the same thing every kid thinks: "When in life am I ever going to use this?"

These very words had come from my daughter's mouth. She wants to be a writer and an artist, even though we have repeatedly driven her past the seedy basement apartment we lived in during the early years of our creative career pursuits. We reminded her that she was born during those years and slept in a closet. She says she doesn't remember. I remember, and truthfully, our income didn't require much math.

But of course, now that I'm grown up and mature and full of regret, I understand the importance of applying yourself passionately to every educational opportunity. I kept telling my daughter, "Even if you never use that useless junk, you are learning how to learn." With this and other poetic gems, I've tried to convince her that education is never a waste. More than mastering the subject itself, the practice of applying herself to something difficult develops important life skills. You should have seen the eye roll. Apparently the phrase *life skills* is a serious buzzword used frequently by faculty and guidance counselors.

For her, *life skills* meant making a quick pass through the hall in time to avoid the glob of gangstas who mark their territory with obscenities and maimed people or scoring a rare flair for her Facebook profile. Geometry offers no application for survival in Teen Town and is therefore pointless.

In desperation, I did the unthinkable. I tried to bring validity to my cause with an experience from my own life. "Though it wasn't my favorite subject in school either, I was surprised to find that I do use geometry as an adult . . . when I make my quilts." I thought her pupils would never return to center position. Knowing she views me as the suffocater of all things fun, I don't know what I thought would be convincing about telling her that junior high math skills will come in handy later when her life is as dull as mine and hunching over a sewing machine for hours is considered entertainment.

Determined to persevere, we set the mandate that her math homework had to be checked nightly by her dad. We concluded that while my skills in geometry for quilting were adept, they probably did not qualify me beyond fabric use. So night after night, the two of them sat at the kitchen table working the numbers. I quilted nearby to offer subliminal support.

In the midst of this battle, my daughter and I found ourselves at a meeting held by the school counselors to register for high school and plan for the future. I was pumped. This was just what my kid needed—a reality check about the competitive world she would face. They began the presentation with a video demonstration called "Did You Know?" Set to a thumping mega-mix and funky graphics, the display showed statistics about future jobs, American education competency versus international statistics, how the information superhighway and technology have exploded and changed everything, and how, by the time their generation finishes a four-year degree, the information and skills they learn will be obsolete and the people of China and India will run the world. They turned off the projector and said, "So let's talk about what you want to be when you grow up."

I wonder who thought it was a good idea to inspire our children by telling them they are receiving a second-rate education and will eventually live like third-world citizens. Though not helpful to my cause, I tried to spin it in my favor. "Wow, that was an eye-opener. Sounds like technology is where the future is, and everybody knows that technology means math."

"Yeah, but it sounds like the Asians have the technology thing covered, so I'll just stick with writing and art."

"Well, then, let's just hope the new techno-global government will value creative outlet."

Meanwhile, we kept her nose to the grindstone and continued to check her progress. We were discouraged to find that our additional effort was not producing results. We were doing everything we knew to do from home, and our daughter assured us she was gathering whatever meager bread crumbs the evil warden dropped in class.

We started to think that maybe our genetic curse was just too much to overcome. Maybe three right-brainers, even with our heads together, would never add up to one left-brain grade. Just when we were about to give up and let her fail and follow her dreams, a spark glimmered. She brought home an A math assignment. She'd done it! In fact, she acknowledged that she was actually understanding the concepts. She was on her way to hobnobbing with the turban gods in designing the technology that would extract creative thought directly from the brain and distribute it throughout the cyber-universe.

Then comes the rain.

She stormed in one day. "I give up! I finally get it, and I get punished anyway. This is why I don't even try. She's so unfair." She threw a math assignment into the air.

We probed for explanation. Apparently, the assignment she had successfully completed with her dad the night before had all the right answers, but she received an F because she had forgotten to label her answers appropriately with inches, centimeters, and so on.

I was livid. Zero credit for a small labeling discrepancy? I started to think that perhaps our faulty gene pool was not completely to blame. Maybe my daughter really had been trying all along, and this teacher was the unreasonable tyrant she described. The movie *Freaky Friday* might actually be on to something. I tried to think if the guy I turned down for senior prom had become a math teacher. No, her teacher was a woman. A witch. No, a spy. A double agent working as part of an underground network of math teachers who serve foreign governments to ambush our children into feeling stupid so they can take over the world with their technology. That's it!

Aha. I was on to their scheme, and I would put a stop to it immediately using their own technology against them—e-mail.

From: karirich@bigmomma.net
Subject: Concerned Parent
To: mswhippit@icucoming.org

Dear Ms. Whippit,
As you know, our daughter has been struggling in your class. Since it seems the resources and policies of your class are limited, we have been working with her at home to try to improve her understanding of the concepts and her grades. It has been difficult, but we have been making some headway—until today, when she received zero credit for correct answers that were not labeled correctly. She was extremely discouraged, as were we. I understand the need to be thorough, but it seems that a correct answer should be worth some credit. In a subject that so many students seem to struggle with, it seems every effort should be made by faculty to encourage them and make available the resources they need to help them succeed.

Sincerely—Kari J. Rich

Civil, but direct. I anxiously awaited a sniveling cover-up response.

From: mswhippit@icucoming.org
Subject: The Truth Will Set You Free
To: karirich@bigmomma.net

Dear Mrs. Rich,

I appreciate your concern and effort to help your daughter improve. I realize math is a difficult subject, which is why I have a generous makeup policy and extended office hours for tutoring. All assignments and tests can be reworked for an improved grade, and I'm available before and after school in addition to the study period. I've been surprised your daughter hasn't used these resources or made you aware of them, as I remind my students of them constantly and have thought all year that your daughter is one who could have greatly benefited from them. I appreciate your involvement in your child's education. Let me know if there is anything else I can do for you.

Sincerely,
Ms. Whippit

P.S. Please remind your daughter to leave her leisure reading book in her locker.

Game over. You win.

Ms. Whippit and her underground co-op can have the world. They deserve it. But they might want to consider hiring a few select Generation Z Americans when they've grown up. When building an empire, subterfuge skills can be very handy.

18
Winter Olym-peon

THE LAST TIME THE WINTER Olympics took place, I wondered if the committee, in all their uber-efforts to organize every minor detail of this grand event, remembered to hire good lawyers. Why? Because I thought my daughter was going to sue them. The Winter Olympics were so awesome and addictive and readily available to me via satellite, DVR, internet, and more, that during their broadcasting duration, there was no clean underwear or food in our house. Some might argue that the Olympic committee bears no fault in the fact that I became dead weight in my household from the opening ceremonies to the closing ceremonies postparty. I personally think my daughter had a strong case. I hope she wins a billion dollars so she can pay someone else to take over my household duties permanently. Then I would be free to pursue my dream of becoming an Olympic athlete.

At my age, I know there are going to be limits to what events I can pursue. But curling looks basically like beer-belly ice bowling, and my current occupation has helped me develop mad broom skills and scrubbing forearms. To feel fulfilled, I don't even need a gold medal. I'd even take one of those lesser medals that seem to be a disappointment for some reason. Actually, I'd just be happy to be there wearing spandex, sequins, or mukluks in the mix of the competition. I know it's a long shot, but sitting on my couch for several days gorging myself on Olympic spirit made me dream big . . . and feel small.

Watching montages of "the thrill of victory and the agony of defeat" from subcelestial suburbia has put a mundane magnifying glass on my life. It seems these people are living life large. Sure, there are years of sacrifice, grueling training, injury, disappointments, and all that, but win or lose, these athletes are chasing a dream in the thick of a spectacular, historic event.

There are roaring crowds, waving flags, blazing torches, culture, language, diversity, competition, controversy, rivalry, and revelry. It is life in 4D, and it makes my life look like it could use some WD-40. It makes me feel like all that note writing and passing I did in my teens was probably a waste of time since I should have been doing laps around an ice oval with Dan Jansen. These athletes grabbed life by the horns in their youth. They had a vision of being something and doing something. Now that I'm middle-aged, I have vision, but unfortunately, it's slowly becoming far-sighted.

My life as a mother and homemaker is full of sacrifice, grueling training, injury, and disappointments too, but my podium is the rug in front of the kitchen sink, and the only weighty thing to ever hang around my neck has been a screaming toddler.

I think what I envy most about these Olympians is the feeling of a defining life moment. Being able to experience a sum of a million disciplined decisions encapsulated in one glorious "Ta-da!" That moment doesn't even have to be standing on top of a podium. It could be walking into a stadium wearing a Team USA uniform, waving at a rowdy international crowd. The rush of standing at the top of a foreboding slope, wondering if my life will be completely different at the bottom. Waiting in the middle of an ice rink for the music to start, the eyes of the world looking at me, thinking I might be the next American sweetheart.

America did get a golden sweetheart in the 2010 Winter Olympics. Alpine ski star Lindsey Vonn came into the Olympics with high hopes and an injury that threatened her medal chances. She fought hard and won a gold medal in her first event. She bawled and blurted out, "I've given up everything for this. It means everything to me!" While that is sweet and true on some levels, I don't think she's really missed out on much. She mentioned in an interview that she never got to go to prom. Well, I'll trade her my permed hair, teal taffeta buffoon dress, and dork date for her gold medal. So she missed out on some of the hallmark happenings of youth, like Saturday morning cartoons, junk food fests, and playing "light as a feather stiff as a board" at slumber parties while your bra stiffens in a cup of water in the freezer. Now, while she travels the world, racks up rankings, and shmoozes with the rich and famous,

I'm joining weight loss groups and paying shrinks to stop the *Land of the Lost* nightmares. If Ms. Vonn feels badly that her gold medal training made her miss two hundred *Scooby-Doo* episodes, I can easily catch her up on the suspiciously similar plot formula.

Though my Olympic dreams are pipe dreams, and I don't mean half-pipe dreams with Shaun White, they have inspired me to try to bring spirit to my own daily tasks. Create ta-da moments of my own.

One day I utilized the intercom in my house to make an announcement. "Ladies and gentlemen, Team MOM hopeful Kari Rich has just completed a successful run of laundry, where the clothes were washed, dried, folded, and put away all in the same day! This is a personal best for Kari and makes her the current world champion in this event."

The crowd didn't go wild, unless you count mumbles and moans.

After balancing one last dirty dish in an overstuffed dishwasher, I raised my arms in the air and pumped my fists while yelling, "Yay! I did it! I totally nailed it!"

My family did wave a flag, a white one in the form of a napkin.

I knew there just had to be some way to Olympicize my life. So on a crisp winter morning, I decided to ditch my indoor workout and go for a walk to clear my head and make room for inspiration. I grabbed my daughter's iPod and headed out. As I started trudging up the hill from my house, a song from the 2008 Summer Olympic soundtrack came on. Images filled my head of Michael Phelps gasping for air while spreading his butterfly wings, of golden track shoes and green thigh-huggers on a cocky track god, and of beach volleyball babes caught in unflattering snapshots diving for the ball.

As these images played in my brain, I suddenly realized something amazing was happening . . . I was running. I hate to run. I never run. The only time I run is if there's a death-threatening emergency or I'm going downhill and I'm almost home and I'm feeling fat. But there I was, just having left the house, running uphill no less. Suddenly, I knew the Olympic secret ingredient: the music. What is the best part of the Olympics? Those rockin' montages at the end of the broadcast that recap the day's events. The sappily serenaded "up close and personal" segments about the athletes' lives. Glorious moments in slow-mo set to J-Lo. The right tunes make victory look more victorious and defeat look more defeating. I realized all I needed to ramp up my life was a good soundtrack in the background.

I ran all the way up the hill and back home, singing to my own international audience of wild turkeys, scraggly stray cats, and roaming neighborhood dogs. I arrived back at my house out of breath, with my muscles going spastic from rare exertion, but pumped about my new formula for success. When my eyes cleared, I looked around my house. There were last night's dinner dishes crusting over in the sink, backpacks, coats, and school papers strewn everywhere, days of unopened bills screaming silent due dates, Mount Laundry looming, and a couch full of lounging loadies. Panic rose up and threatened to trump my incarnation.

Then one of the loadies looked up at me and spoke. "Hey, Mom. You look wasted. Come sit and hang with us."

I looked at her, her couch-fellows, and around my house at the evidence of a full and meaningful life and thought, *I've given up everything for this. It means everything to me.* I walked over, flipped on the stereo, and cranked up the volume. "All right, Team RICH. Time to make some toilets shine like gold!"

19
Scout-O-Mama

I GREW UP SMACK IN the middle of a slew of sisters, so the world of Scouting was new to me when my son turned eight and became an official Cub Scout. It was baptism by fire into the program because right out of the gate, I was asked to be den mother of my son's Wolf Pack. I quickly realized the titles and symbolism used in Scouting are literal. The first day nine rowdy hooligans stormed my house, the use of a toothy carnivore as their mascot seemed perfectly suiting. They sniffed around every inch of my den, growled for food, and barked orders at me. I quickly promoted myself to den dictator and laid down the law.

First, upon entering the den, they would remove their shoes and go wash their filthy paws. Second, they were only allowed in the areas of the den designated for the activity. Third, if they exhibited signs of human evolution in the form of manners, they could have a portion of the kill-of-the-day snack I provided for them. They howled a little but eventually put their tails between their legs and complied.

Over time, signs of civilization emerged in my little pack as they learned skills, passed off requirements, earned badges, and occasionally even sat still and listened. But every wolf pack has a black sheep. One cub persisted in blatant disruption. He used terms I didn't know until I was married, created harmonies out of bodily sounds, and spouted cynical sarcasm that made me look like an amateur. Worst of all, his favorite expression was, "That is so stupid." Though a simple expression, it was contaminating our pack like poison.

Eight-year-old boys can be rambunctious and overly articulate in bathroom humor, yet they still possess a sweet innocence and are pretty easy to please. For the most part, my cubs took an eager interest in whatever we were doing, until they heard the words, "That is so stupid." Even though they are preteen, peer pressure does apply. Instantly, the painted rocks they were so proud of moments before were discarded in the dirt. The obstacle course they had just conquered became an array of objects to ransack. The badge they had just earned turned into a miniature Frisbee. He had to be stopped. But how?

The handling of such a situation in a volunteer organization is tricky. He isn't my kid, so I couldn't just smack him around. In fact, the front of every Scout manual contains a comprehensive epistle on the serious consequences of abuse within the Scout organization. I checked it over thoroughly, hoping to find a "bratty kid clause," but there were unfortunately no exceptions. I tried timeouts, tongue lashings, and snack deprival—all of which were met with looks and stances that said, "Is that all you got, lady?" Though positioned as a dictator, I was self-promoted, so I didn't know if I had the authority to banish him. If he kept showing up, I guess I had to do my best to teach him. So I decided on a new tactic—ignore him.

The day we made birdhouses as a den made me realize that someone in the Scouting administration has a sick sense of humor. We are supposed to take every precaution to protect our precious Scouts from abuse, but to fulfill Requirement #17d, we're supposed to give them hammers, drills, and saws, and let them run amuck. As the activity progressed, it became perfectly apparent to me that only someone with perfect patience—like Jesus—could be a carpenter. We assembled wood blocks with screws and nails and reassembled boys with band-aids and stitches. The wolf in black sheep's clothing was up to his usual antics, but I gave him no attention and no access to power tools, so he spent the afternoon chucking his wood blocks at the wall.

As the activity wrapped up, each Scout took a turn displaying his handiwork for the pack. Seeing my own son's gigantic grin and puffed-out chest as he held up the lopsided birdhouse that would provide a steady stream of bird seed onto our patio was worth every purple fingernail I'd acquired that day.

Cue the villain. "That is so stupid."

The other boys started laughing, and my son's grin faded, and his chest deflated as he set his masterpiece down and shrugged, trying to act like he didn't care about it anymore.

And then I revealed the true law of the pack—don't mess with den mother and her cub by birth.

I walked up to the kid and put my alpha female nose in his face. "Since you think Scouting is so stupid, why don't I just take you home right now? Go get your pile of blocks, get in my car, and we'll go up to your door together and tell your mom that the only thing you made today was another Scout feel stupid. We'll tell her all the jokes you like to share and have you perform the symphonies you compose with your armpit. Then she'll know why you don't want to come to Scouts anymore because she'll see that everything you do here is so stupid."

He stood stunned. For once, he had no comeback. I took my car keys out of my pocket and shook them in his face. The other pack members froze, uncertain if they were in trouble too. His expression slowly turned to that of a pup whose nose had just been swatted with a newspaper.

After several awkward seconds, he whimpered, "I want to stay."

I held my position. "You want to stay? You want to stay and do stupid things with us?"

Whispered response. "They're not stupid."

"What? I didn't hear that."

Slightly louder. "They're not stupid."

I wouldn't let him off so easily. "I think I heard you that time, but I don't think anyone else here did. Speak up, Scout."

"They're not stupid!"

Satisfied, I called off the dog. "All right, then. You give me a proud Scout salute and go join your den brothers."

He saluted me, which is probably sacrilege since I think Scouts are only supposed to salute the flag, but it seemed appropriate in the moment to complete the point. I'll have to check the manual to see if I was supposed to submit a "breach of conduct" report about it or ceremoniously rip a patch off my sleeve. Anyway, den activity resumed without further incident—for the day, at least.

So you're probably wondering if my den demon changed. He did. He turned nine and changed dens. I wonder how he'll fare in the den of mother bear?

20
Heaven Self-Help Me

OPRAH CALLED IT QUITS. THE great and powerful Wizard of O got into her hot air balloon and floated back to wherever she came from before we bowed to her, clamoring for brains and hearts. This announcement sent Americans into a tizzy. *Where will we find truth now? Who will inform us about the latest diet, the private lives of Hollywood's A-list, and the dangers of store-bought eggs? How will we know what books to read, which cosmetics have high toxin levels, or how to dress to flatter a pear-shaped figure?* I can only imagine the pressure the network suits were under to search the skies for the next great guru.

After all, self-help is big business these days. Everybody is an expert on something and has developed some system, program, diet, workshop, seminar, life plan, support group, book, or blog to help the general public with everything from organizing a broom closet to cleansing your colon to marrying a millionaire.

I admit I have dipped my ladle into the self-help well many times. As a youth, I was fiercely independent, overly confident, and ready to ride atop a tornado to my own dreams located somewhere over the rainbow. I left home at eighteen, ready to show my parents I did know everything and was ready to live my own life.

Then my own life began.

I started college and realized I had no idea what I really wanted to do. I got a job and found out my college education did not adequately prepare me for the corporate world. I got married, having no clue how to be a wife. I got pregnant and realized I had no idea how to raise the being that would eventually work its way out of me. I got fat and realized the habits of eating and exercise I'd fostered in my youth would not sustain a healthy or lengthy adulthood. I bought a house with a yard and a garden, which revealed my lack of household and yard management skills. Starting a home business unveiled my novice knowledge of tax laws, marketing, time management, bookkeeping, retirement plans, health insurance, life insurance . . .

How did life get so complicated so fast? I had completed seventeen years of formal education, yet I was a human survival invalid. Each new stage of life revealed more stuff I didn't know. Where do I turn? Who will teach me what I need to know? How do I know what is truth? Where's Yoda?

Since my self-help quest began prehistorically (i.e., pre-www), I had to rely on the printed page. I found out from a friend that Yoda's lair was called Borders. I walked through the double doors, and my second education began. "And when the woman saw that the tree was good . . . and a tree to be desired to make one wise, she took of the fruit thereof, and did eat" (Genesis 3:6).

I think Borders is a very misleading name. The word *borders* suggests that there is an end somewhere, a limit. As I gazed across the never-ending aisles and stacks of books, I quickly realized there is no border around the amount of advice and/or number of people ready to tell you how to live your life. I was intimidated and fascinated at the same time. I glanced at some of the titles and authors and opened a few books to read snippets and inside cover matter. The collection of experts ranged from decorated scholars, philosophers, doctors, and business titans to witch doctors, bohemians, recovered burn-outs, and regular shmoes. Overwhelmed by the varying selection and opposing approaches to conquer life, I opted to start small in my quest to clean up my life. I decided to start with my complexion.

If this sounds shallow . . . it is. I just wasn't ready to develop six habits of hyperactive humans or learn the proper burping and care of husbands yet. Being a recovering pride monger, I knew I would have to take baby steps up the mountain, and pimples seemed like an elevation I could handle. I bought a book that promised it contained the cure for acne. Since this was the beginning of my self-help journey, I was still naïve enough to believe words like *cure, absolute, promise*, and *for life*.

Like any program, there was a strict regimen to be followed to get results. Part of the process was to apply a generous amount of benzoyl peroxide over the affected area then place a cold pack on it for twenty minutes. This sounded simple enough if your problem was a basic T-zone, but mine was from the waist up. The book did suggest that if you have multiple problem areas, you could treat them one at a time. Did I mention that in addition to being insufferably independent, I also struggle with impatience? If I followed the prescribed regiment for each area of my body that needed attention, I could have been completely cleared up in time to receive my senior discount. No go. I had swallowed my pride and jumped on the wagon, and I wanted results pronto.

After trying to finagle several ice packs in sundry places on myself, I started pricing the cost of installing a meat locker I could stand naked in for twenty minutes a day. I discovered that meat lockers were expensive, especially without the butcher discount. I was left to my own resources, which can be surprisingly innovative yet frightening.

The use of regular rectangular ice packs worked well enough for flatter anatomy, but the face and neck have many awkward angles, and I was partial to being able to breathe during the cold incubation period. A brilliant idea cognated. Using my crude sewing skills, some table cover plastic, and the blue goo extracted from several ice packs, I designed and assembled an all-inclusive, one-of-a-kind, frozen H_2O headgear. I was ecstatic as I positioned my concoction over myself and reclined on my bed to lay waste adult acne. When my husband walked in and viewed the prone popsicle, he declared, "This gives a whole new meaning to being frigid in bed."

Despite my valiant efforts, the frosty formula did not turn out to be my cure for acne. The involved regimen proved too time-consuming for consistency, and my skin and marriage were suffering from freezer burn. Yes, my first self-help venture was a bust. Oh, but I still had so very many exploits that awaited me.

There was the time during a postpartum nesting bout that I was so desperate to regain some sense of order that I bought a book written by a woman who professed to be a happily organized homemaker. A modern model of June Cleaver, she boasted five children, a clean house, and an orderly schedule—all completed with a wink and a smile. I worked feverishly to be a worthy disciple. But by day five into the regimen, I was already a mopping day delinquent, three laundry loads behind, and I had thrown more tantrums than my toddler. The only activity I completed on schedule was the ceremonial burning of her book.

Perhaps my biggest contribution to the self-help industry is my generous sponsorship of the parenting biz. There is big pressure to be a good parent these days. What you say or do—or don't say or do—eat, drink, or teach your offspring from inception to legal age will decide whether you sit in the stands at the Olympics or the gallery of a courtroom.

Wanting to give my children every opportunity to succeed in life and avoid being the antagonist of the *Mommy Dearest* sequel, I gorged on parenting prose. I tried every system, program, style, and chart available, trying to find the formula that would produce the brilliant, obedient automatons I desired. The problem was, I had filled my brain with so many options I couldn't remember which one I was on when a parenting conundrum surfaced. Was I *Parenting with Love and Logic* now or practicing *Tough Love*? Had I harnessed *The Power of Positive Parenting* yet, or was I still in *Parenting 101*? In such moments, my children would prompt me with reminders.

"Mom, aren't you supposed to be practicing *Scream-free Parenting* now?"

"YES! WHY DO YOU HAVE TO STINKIN' ASK???!!!"

Probably a close second to parenting self-help would be the numerous sources I've tapped about diet and exercise. Oh, the volumes I could fill with those dark tales. A dingy cupboard full of odd appliances, a shelf stacked with unsavory recipe books, a storage room corner where exercise contraptions and a stack of VHS Tae Bo lurk, and my closet full of clothes ranging in sizes from six to sixteen all groan in agony when these tales surface, so I'll abstain.

Yes, in my quest for self-improvement, I have worshiped at many altars, most of which have gone up in smoke. At first, I blamed myself. I just wasn't disciplined enough, motivated enough, or organized enough. Then I blamed the industry. Maybe like The Great and Powerful Oz, it's all just a show of smoke and mirrors. I had bought into the idea that some wizard had the answers for me. I had gone to self-help and back only to discover that perhaps behind the curtain lurked a sniveling fraud.

But Dorothy does eventually get her wish. Despite the fact that she risks her life to retrieve the broom of her arch nemesis only to bring it back to lay it at the feet of a fake, she does get what she wants in the end. How did she do it?

Dorothy's journey down the yellow brick road of self-discovery was similar to mine. She looked around at her world and wanted to be someone and somewhere better. Then after spending days of odd adventure with a flock of freaks, she discovered all she wanted was to get back home, which is really where I want my self-help journey to take me. Home to a place where I lived before with a Being much, much greater than any wizard. Home to a place within myself that is comfortable with who I am while I work at becoming worthy to get back to Him. Like Dorothy, there are some off-beat ideas and people I've latched onto in my quest, but even they have served in the growth process.

And so, Dorothy does get home. After putting all her faith and effort into the idea that someone else has all the answers, she discovers that she possessed the power to help herself all along—in her heart and on her feet. I do too. Never underestimate the power of a great pair of shoes.

21
Camp Wannasmackagirl

"WHEN I AM WEARY, I go to the mountains."

A friend quoted this serene thought while we were sitting around a campfire on the last night of ward girls camp. She had just arrived at dusk that evening and was basking in the revelry of glowing embers under a night sky sprayed with stars and framed by towering pines. I sat next to her with my aching limbs sprawled across a crippled camp chair and stared up into the universe with a glazed expression, and I wondered where I had gone wrong.

As camp director, I had just spent three days trying to beat a love of the great outdoors into twenty teenage girls while simultaneously staving off a leader mutiny. The mountains had failed me. My friend's quote suggested sanctuary—an escape from the world where one could unplug and commune with nature. Apparently, even Mother Nature has limits on how much estrogen she can accommodate at one time.

In my lifetime, I have gone to eleven girls camps: five times as a youth and six times as camp director. The first time I was called to lead this annual event, I thought it was because of my natural leadership skills, my playful yet spiritual personality combo, and the active/outdoorsy lifestyle I exude. Then a few months later, I found myself driving the highway in a panic, searching for a girl who had spouted a dark cloud of profanity at me then run into the woods threatening to hitchhike home—and I realized the real reason I was called. I'm a chump.

The ward probably throws the biggest party of the year the week they send their teenage daughters into the mountains. The girls' parents party the hardest, leading out in limbo contests and belting out Barry Manilow karaoke tunes such as "Looks Like We Made It!" Meanwhile, in the depths of the forest, the clueless few called to cover camp huddle together shivering in a dark tent while scenes from *The Crucible* play out nearby.

I loved girls camp as a kid. At twelve years old, I saw it as my first parent-free week away from home, and I felt all grown up and independent, even if I did have to dig my own latrine. Back in those good ol' days, you could still pull playful pranks and initiation rituals without ending up in the news.

My first year of camp, the junior leaders tied all seventeen of us new Beehives together wrist to wrist to spend an entire night. Eating tinfoil dinners proved comical as we tried to fork hobo cuisine with an extra flopping appendage. The lefties were screwed. Brushing our teeth became a game of facial paste smearing and laughter-invoked foam spewing. We were allowed to untie one hand long enough to "take care of business." I can still see the long line of us standing outside the ajar outhouse door while a wrist-mate yelled, "Stop looking!" Most of us decided to hold it until morning.

When I finally became a junior leader, my cohorts and I were ready to pay it all forward. Though restrictions were beginning to tighten, we found creative uses for rubber snakes and spiders and still managed to raise the colors in the form of a pink, lacey double A.

It is a little known fact that the best local cultural fair takes place on the down-low of campgrounds after dark. Skits showcasing girls dressed in kimonos and rainbow afro wigs belting out modified Beatles lyrics while leaping across lantern-lit amphitheater stages are not to be missed. One time, for a military-themed camp, we held a G.I. Jane pageant. Contestants had to use items from a bag filled with random sundries given to them right before the show. For the talent competition, a set of tiny blonde twins squeezed into one pant leg each of a giant pair of pants and creatively demonstrated the Heimlich maneuver. They were definite frontrunners until one of them lost their balance.

Then there's the food. Oh, the food. Everything tasted better when you put it on a stick and torched it over a campfire with your friends. The dark, seductive side of the Stay Puft Man, the Pillsbury Doughboy, and the Keebler Elves is revealed by firelight. We wrapped marshmallows in biscuits and rolled them in butter, sugar, and cinnamon. We swirled breadstick dough around wieners and doused the toasty, mummified pigs with chili. We stuffed roasted marshmallows between Fudge Shoppe Deluxe Grahams™, Fudge Stripes™ shortbreads, peanut butter filled cookies, and anything else those wicked elves concocted for evil pleasure. We passed out in sugar comas on our sleeping bags, with melted marshmallows slathered across our stoned faces. We slept guilt-free as our teenage metabolisms ravaged the calories like an inferno, saving just enough to burn off during the thigh-busting hike the next day.

But with the sweet does comes the bitter . . . drama.

Shakespeare's got nothin' on girls camp. You cannot bring a group of teenage girls and an array of women leaders, from twenty-something to postmenopausal, and not have several well-played acts of both comedy and tragedy. There are tent assignment tantrums, "They're leaving me out" tears, secret sister confusion and envy, clothes stealing, make-up hiding, and "That's not fair" feuds. Distinctive battles erupt from opposing parties like the princesses vs. the tree huggers, the fear-factor snarfers vs. the diva dieters, and the classic Mollies vs. the rebels. And that's just the girls. Just when you think teenagers have reached the pinnacle of immature behavior, two grown women start trash-talking over superior dutch oven recipes.

When I would tell my husband the gory details of forest feline fighting, he would shake his head and say, "I'm glad I'm a guy. It's so much simpler just to beat on the shmuck till he stops."

"Till he stops what?" I queried.

"Either being a shmuck or breathing."

Simpler indeed.

There is a big difference between being a participant and being the Grand Poobah of camp. There are good times to be had at camp even as a leader—like the time the Young Women president and I got in trouble with the stake leaders for cliff jumping. "Name That Ward Member" charades in the leader tent by night is a gut buster, and spray bottle wake-up calls for early morning flag ceremony are a blast. Unlimited access to the s'more supplies is also a nice perk. But having been in charge six times, there are definitely times when I think a swinging clenched fist would have produced an exhilarating release.

It's lonely at the top. When the rain pours down, confining all to the close quarters of drenched tents, they look to you for creative uses of Uno cards. Enforcing a sentence on a girl required to wear the "modesty muumuu" for breaching dress standards is like cursing her with the pox. You find yourself as the deciding vote during a private leader powwow that determines whether or not to send the girl home who freely shared her level of intimacy experience with a tent full of wide-eyed Beehives. You duck into your car to have a good cry when you overhear your fellow leaders talking about how lame camp has been this year.

Whether a young woman or a seasoned sister, time in the wilderness does provide a prime setting for learning life lessons, which is what I think was God's intention. In the scriptures, whenever the Lord wanted to teach His people something important, He sent them into the wilderness—the Israelites, Lehi's family, the brother of Jared, the pioneer trek west, Zion's Camp, and so on. There's something about being away from civilization that quickly reveals our true colors. Quarters are close, responsibilities are big, and you have to learn to get along, figure it out, and do your part because excuses and diversions are few. When conditions are crude, emotions become raw, and sometimes the situation explodes. Let us not forget the beating Nephi took, and he was hardly the group shmuck.

When I was a youth, I thought girls camp was about learning survival skills. Now as an adult, I know it is, but it has little to do with starting a fire with flint and steel. It's seeing if your testimony is strong enough to face fellow leaders the Sunday following camp and smile and forgive when just days before they had staged a coup. It's checking your patience and unconditional love levels while scrubbing vomit out of your car; off of sleeping bags, pillows, and blankets; and out of the hair of a violently hurling Mia Maid. It's choosing your words carefully when the bishop asks why a leader turned in a receipt from an auto body shop and declared it a camp expense.

In the midst of gathering coolers and tents, planning meals, rehearsing skits, and teaching how to tie a half hitch, I've learned to be organized, prayerful, creative, humble, frugal, obedient, cooperative, and a whole other slew of characteristics that are going to come in handy in life and the eternities. Of course, it's given me immeasurable gratitude for the leaders who patiently tolerated and taught me in the wilderness of my youth, grooming me to be of service in the kingdom long before I knew I would be called to do so.

Eventually, my turn to stand and say something profound by the fire comes. I close my sleep-deprived eyes and pray for inspiration. I stand and say, "Over the years at camp, I've watched girls struggle to master wilderness survival skills. When they get overwhelmed, the most common question I get is, 'When am I ever going to use this in real life?' My answer is always . . . I don't know. But if you end up like me, it might be eleven more times than you expected."

22
The Family Business

THE EXPRESSION "FAMILY BUSINESS" HAS various meanings. For some people, "family business" means they have decided to further complicate the high emotions of living under the same roof by leaving that roof and reconvening at the same-DNA-established workplace to bounce off of each other some more. If you're Italian, "family business" might mean buying a violin just for the case and being suspicious of what's in your ravioli. For those of us who don't have the luxury of mafia connections or nepotism, "family business" is the private, delicate matters of home life to be entrusted only amongst ourselves and Dr. Laura. But if you're clever, the line between these differing definitions can be blurred for fame and gain when personal experiences are exposed.

I went to see the play *The Glass Menagerie*, by Tennessee Williams. I was feeling all cultured, carefree, and kid-free as I cozied into my velvet theater seat and casually scanned the program. My high school AP English teacher had been thorough, so I was, years later, still vaguely familiar with the play and other famous works by Mr. Williams. I read the engaging synopsis, noting that the playwright based characters on himself and family members. I settled in for the complexities of family drama, anxious to see which branches of the Williams' family tree didn't fork.

The cast was excellent, and I marveled at the brilliant literary quality of the dialogue and narration, but as the play progressed, I became increasingly unsettled. The fact that Tennessee was a prodigy born out of dysfunction was apparent. Not surprising. Many of the great ones gotta lotta coo-coo from the crib. But the portrayal of one character particularly bothered me. At the center of the play was a flighty, overbearing, delusional mother. Knowing the character was based on

Tennessee's own mother, I was irked by the representation. We all find our own therapeutic formats to deal with family issues, but putting on a tuxedo and selling tickets to the premier of *My Mother Was a Quack and Ruined My Life* seemed uncalled for.

I realize maternal instincts kicked in, and I probably took the portrayal too personally. I concede that the mother, Amanda, was high maintenance, but her history offered some justification. She grew up in a fluffy world of privilege as a Southern debutante. Although Amanda was wooed by a flock of wealthy Southern gentlemen, a handsome traveling salesman solicited exceptional charm and closed the deal on her heart. She left the bubble behind with only eyelash batting and gown swishing as life skills. When the realities of life set in—that charm can't compensate for—Mr. Hustle hit the road for an indefinite sales call, leaving Amanda to care for two children. Yes, in her desperate situation, she developed practices that mingled her pretty past with rotten reality and surfaced as darn-you-taunt. Social graces got Amanda into this mess and, by golly, they were going to get her children out of it.

So Amanda told her son to sit up straight. She told him to eat his vegetables, chew his food before swallowing, get more sleep, and tell her where he was going late at night. She told him to stop wasting his time in movies and bars. She told him to bring home eligible friends so she could shmooze them with Southern hospitality and introduce them to her lovely but odd and reclusive daughter of marriageable age. No one is denying that some of her methods revealed a crack in her Crock-Pot, but she did the best she could with what she had.

The portrait pricked a nerve in me because some of the nagging dialogue rang too familiar. *Is that how I sound? Am I like that? Will my children grow up to be bitter and resentful and use dinner theater as a psychological outlet?* My mind began cataloging my children's creative catharses. I have one daughter who draws nothing but dragons. *Do they all have hazel eyes?* My other daughter reads, writes, and draws strictly fantasy. *Is that her anti-mommy alternate universe?* My son likes soccer. *Is the ball my head?* I hated Tennessee! How dare he air out his dirty laundry on stage. How dare he write plays from Freud's couch and publicly point a finger at the woman who gave him life and only wanted proper digestion and posture for her son. I can't remember what I thought of Williams' work when my teenage brain had tried to absorb high-frequency literature. I probably would have thought, "That lady is a freak. Get over yourself and lay off already."

But now it was different. I am a Mrs. Williams of sorts. I haven't been abandoned by my husband (yet), and I was raised Western scrapper rather than Southern debutante. But I'm a mom, and I tell my kids to eat their vegetables, sit up straight, and tell me the truth about where they go and what they do. I encourage them to have goals and aspirations that will eventually get them out of my house and provide funds for my luxurious suite in a senility ward. Shame on you, Tennessee Williams! Since you sold out and cashed in on your mother's insanity, I hope her grave is marked with a very expensive headstone.

A few days after attending the play, I witnessed a contrasting family sample. At a writers' conference, I listened as a successful new author and daughter of a world-renowned self-help guru raved about her brilliant upbringing, crediting the application of her father's principles as key to her success. The father offered a brief cameo at the end of her remarks, brimming with pride over his trophy of accomplished parenting. I was about to retch in solidarity for Mrs. Williams and every other malfunctioning mother when these two family displays collided in my brain.

As father and daughter gushed and hugged all the way to the bank, I suddenly stopped hating Tennessee Williams. I quit feeling sorry for his mother. I realized that the parenting end result was the same in both cases, wasn't it? The trophy child and Ursula's offspring both achieved success, didn't they? I suddenly realized I could stop contributing to my kids' trust funds. I could tear up the frivolous will that divvies up the residue of my pathetic life. What was I so worried about? Whether I possess the Midas touch or poison apple of parenting, my creative spawn can exploit whatever junk I fill their brains and behaviors with and make a truckload! Whether my kids hit the circuit with the gothic novel *Reign of Dark Mummy* or produce the musical *Kari the Good Fairy*, they'll get to meet Rachel Ray, right?

So let the dragons fly! Let the fantasy novels flow! Kick the ball, baby, because our family is open for business!

.

23
Tapped Out

I HAVE WONDERFUL FRIENDS, SUPPORTIVE, motivated people who bring out the best in me and push me to improve myself. That's why I gotta dump 'em. I think I need to surround myself with cynical fat slugs who have no interest in encouraging me to grow as a person. You'd think after the triathlon ordeal I would have learned my lesson, but I'm apparently extremely malleable in the hands of productive peers.

A dear friend of mine had this brilliant idea to get together a group of moms and take a tap class. "It will be fun," she said. "We'll send our kids off to school and go pretend to be Ginger Rogers for an hour a week." Stars filled my head. I am a classic musical junky, and she knows it. You see how these people work? I open my heart, my home, and my life to them, and in return, they relentlessly take advantage of my vulnerabilities. I realize now that if I'm going to have close friends, I need to keep the relationship much more formal.

I should never have revealed that I've seen every Esther Williams movie ever made, that I dream about Howard Keel, and that I can sing "S'wonderful, S'marvelous" word for word. My friend has seen the collector's edition set of *That's Entertainment* hosted by Gene Kelly in my closet and is privy to the fact that I bought one hundred and fifty dollar tickets two nights in a row to see *Thoroughly Modern Millie* in New York. She knows I've media time-warped my family badly enough that my husband has mentioned in public how hot Cyd Charisse is. Does she also know that while vacuuming I play portions of the *American in Paris* ballet? Probably. She's just the kind of concerned friend who would let herself into my house if I didn't answer and she knew I was home just to make sure I was okay and catch me midleap.

Anyway, I was sufficiently duped by the idea. I pictured myself busting a retro-move with Donald O'Connor to "Moses supposes his toeses are roses" and agreed. I thought it would be good to challenge myself, to keep my mind and body sharp with new feats of coordination. I figured it was better than eventually ending up on the back of a flatbed truck during a parade, wearing gingham and swishing petticoats as I do-si-do around the senior citizen square. I was unaware I could participate in activities far more disparaging.

Whoever coined the phrase "the old soft shoe" should be flogged. It makes tap dancing sound like any suave cat can become a hoofer with a casual shuffle. I do relate to the term *hoofer*, as cow and/or billy goat images easily come to mind when I watch myself tap in the mirror. Learning tap made me discover I would have to use muscles in my foot I didn't know existed. As I'd sat in my basement shoving popcorn into my face and watching fabulous Fred glide effortlessly, emitting syncopated sounds from his patent leather lace-ups, I was naïve to the depth of coordination and flexibility required for choreographed tapping.

Early on in the class, I realized I would have to make some hard choices. I could be coordinated and quiet or clunky and clumsy and actually produce tapping noises. I chose the latter, and I think my teacher has mixed feelings about my choice. My teacher is amazing, by the way. She's a generation beyond us, yet she is agile, beautiful, and still Broadway-worthy with her skills. The top of her body lilts and sways lightly while mad tap sounds somehow burst from her feet. She has a reputable dance studio that boasts an array of youthful dance hopefuls. Whatever possessed her to go slumming to humor the fantasies of a motley crew of middle-aged moms is beyond me. Even sisterly solidarity has its limits.

However, our class does have its pets. My friend, the ringleader, emerged as an early favorite. Though she swears she never learned tap, she has years of ballet and jazz experience and took to tapping with ease. Another class member was a victim of the 80s clogging craze, which gives her a literal leg-up, though she's had to give up her hitch kick. Two of the other ladies are former drill team members, and though bump and grind aren't typical tap repertoire, it may serve them well in distracting from what their feet can't do. I am a former cheerleader, which means all I can do is shake my pom-poms.

I originally agreed to this venture in order to pay homage to my heroes of the silver screen and keep myself young, or so I thought. But when I forget the steps we've gone over a million times, I panic that it's revealing early signs of Alzheimer's. Teetering with nausea after only two spins proves that my equilibrium has lost its center, and I have nightmares of lying helplessly on a tile floor yelling, "Help, I've fallen, and I can't get up!" So week after week, I tap and twirl, I forget and flail, and I wonder why I willingly signed up to discover that I'm physically and mentally deteriorating faster than I thought and that I'm inadequate at yet another thing in life.

I blame my friends. If they really loved me, they would let me wallow in my static inability. They would tell me they are about to go do something cool, creative, and fulfilling—then ditch me. After all, what are friends are for?

24
Old Dog, New Tricks

FOR SOME STRANGE REASON, WHEN you're young, you don't think you'll ever get old. Even though each birthday celebrates becoming a year older, you still think you'll be immune to becoming wrinkly, careful, boring, and behind. In my cheeky youthful years, I even took part in poking fun of the quirks of the golden-aged.

On a summer morning, my sister and I sat by the side of the pool with our kids and shared several guffaws about the senior water aerobics class going on nearby. As they bobbed up and down, we made humorous commentary about funny rubber caps with chin straps, the various hues of blue and purple hair set in pin curls, and neon floral print swimwear with generously pleated skirts that would never compensate for what they were trying to cover. We laughed and snorted and thought we were so funny. Then my sister said jovially, "Hey, someday that will be us."

We stopped laughing. Suddenly, it wasn't that funny anymore.

I've always thought I would stay young by keeping savvy about changing times. I like new places and faces and shaking things up in my life. But there is an area of the present and future that makes me feel like a Smuckers centurion—technology. One day I spent the afternoon with a charitable soul who agreed to help me set up a website. She was only about ten years younger than I am, but I felt like I needed a pacemaker for my brain as she attempted to tutor me into the new millennium. I had a flashback of trying to teach my mom how to run our first VCR.

I used to think old people let themselves get behind because they are stubborn and set in their ways and won't even try to keep up. While that may be true for some, I'm beginning to think that the saying, "You can't teach an old dog new tricks" contains truth and that I'm unfortunately more of a mature mutt than I thought. I wanted to understand what my friend was trying to teach me. I tried to concentrate, focus and absorb the information. She lost me several times when she spoke in acronym. I asked her for a pen and paper so I could take notes. Her reply made me feel like I'd just asked for a stone tablet and nail. "Umm, I type everything directly into my phone or computer, so I don't really keep that kind of stuff around." Even pens and paper are out. I'm techno-toast.

I'm not completely behind the times. I shop and bank online, use e-mail, and have gone paperless for many things. But I still make handwritten to-do and grocery lists, keep a traditional calendar, and use my cell phone in the antiquated manner of communicating using my voice and ears.

My children take to new technology with ease. They mess around with all the apps I never use on my phone and master any new electronic device, program, or game within minutes of acquisition. I think the younger generations are born with a microchip already installed in their brains. It's not that I'm against having a tech-streme makeover. The spirit is willing, but the brain is weak. I blame it on the fact that I've been the victim of Murphy's Law of technology timing.

It all started upon entering college when the computer age was still in its infancy. The university I attended was founded as an agricultural school, so the most up-to-date technology on campus was a milking machine. Most of the professors had received their education in the dunce cap era and were scrambling to modernize themselves. I chose the university because of its reputation in the arts. I wanted to study advertising and design, and the ranked department boasted an impressive résumé of successful alumni. But I should have checked the expiration date on the professors. Unbeknownst to me, the department had entered a cocoon period to metamorphose into the computer design age. Several of the major professors were on sabbatical learning computer design application to bring back to the department. The dinosaurs left behind to hold up the fort were tenure, close to retirement, and well aware they wouldn't need computer design skills in their lifetime. Naïvely, I enrolled and entered *The Land of the Lost*.

The computer age was cusping; meanwhile, I was learning how to use a stat camera and typesetter and create layouts with dye markers. A few Renaissance folks in my classes were teaching themselves on design programs, and computer-generated assignments started popping up. Our department head, Professor T. Rex, was enraged. In his prime, he had pioneered one of the most successful programs in the country. This new creature of evolution called "computer" made him feel obsolete and old, so he fought against it. He lectured us that computer use for design was a fad that would quickly pass. It would not replace the time-honored methods that had put his program and protégés on the map. To solidify his cause, he introduced a new policy—anyone who turned in assignments containing computer-produced elements would fail. Not only was I in a department lagging behind the times, but advancement was now punishable by "F."

As my senior year approached, I started doing some job market research in order to prepare my portfolio. What I found made me cry. Every entry-level position available listed several computer design program requirements for applicants. I knew none of them. Prof. Rex had failed us. For the price of his pride, he had put us in a cave and taught us how to hieroglyph. I had just put three years and thousands of dollars into an unmarketable degree.

I called him on it. Though a pup, I went toe to toe with the dalai lama of design and told him what I thought of him and his prehistoric pride. He fired back with threats, but I wasn't afraid of him. What could he do to me? Take back my useless education? I stormed out of his department and managed to scrape together enough classes and computer design skills to get an internship that saved my education and my career. I enjoyed a successful stint in an advertising agency that was on the cutting-edge of computer design at the time. But after a few years, it was time for a new design project for me—creating life.

I left the corporate world of design to devote myself to home and family. I tried to keep up my professional skills with occasional freelance projects, but keeping up with technology *and* poopy diapers gets tricky. The bad-timing fairy strikes again. While I was trying to keep my head above laundry, the design world went www. Now I'm finally ready to reboot, but my brain is so full of to-do lists and parenting fodder, it won't absorb any new data.

I understand how Prof. Rex felt. (But I still hate him.) Feeling like the world has left you behind is rotten. But I refuse to roll over and play dead with new technology. This old dog will attempt to learn the new tricks. Even if the road to advancement is ruff.

25
Bette Knows Best

I've always thought Bette Midler was a little sappy. I saw *Beaches*, and I bawled at the end, but I think Bette ruined a perfectly good theme song by milking the ending with all that "fly, fly, fly" nonsense. Shortly after the syrupy success of "Wind beneath My Wings," Bette belted out another deep thoughts tune called "From a Distance." While I thought the message was legitimate, jam is better on toast than by the spoonful. Even though I haven't missed Ms. Midler since Luther Vandross took over as bleeding heart balladeer, an experience summoned the sap in me, bringing the lyrics of "From a Distance" to mind.

I was out on my bike on the familiar roads I ride every day. The early spring air was fresh and moist from the rain, and the neon green hills combined with the snowcapped mountains made me feel like I was back on the Austrian bike tour I took a few years ago. What added to the simile was the view I caught of a house in the distance standing isolated on a hill below the massive peaks. The house was a stately Victorian with steep-pitched roofs, towers, and terraces, and combined with the lush landscape, the scene could easily have been mistaken as one of the many castles I saw nestled in the European countryside. I smiled at the resemblance and worked to keep the beautiful illusion going in my mind since I've suffered lederhosen longing since returning home.

But all too quickly, my mind betrayed me and recalled the reality of that house. I'd been there many times. It was the home of a friend of mine who has been chronically ill and homebound for several years. The mirage and my smile faded as I thought of her in the upper tower room, lying in a bed, trying to keep occupied with sedentary activities to avert her mind from the constant pain. I thought of the disrepair that had overtaken the house and property, since the family's time is much occupied by her constant care. The fantasy far gone now, I wondered how I ever could have mistaken the scene as something idyllic and beautiful when I knew so intimately its coarseness. Then I realized what had allowed me to momentarily view the scene in a different context—distance.

My view had always been from inside the house—by her bed, looking at the clutter, the rows of medicine bottles, and the slow-ticking clock on the wall. All I could see was waste, pain, and suffering. All I could feel was frustration and helplessness as I looked out her window at the world she was missing. I didn't think any other view of this situation could possibly exist, but now I saw differently.

From far away, I couldn't see the peeling paint or growing weeds. I couldn't see the pain in her eyes or her frail frame. While it is good to have been close enough to the situation to learn compassion, empathy, and service, it is also important to step back and view her situation from a distance, the way her Maker sees it.

Heavenly Father knows the end from the beginning. He sees everything and everyone from a heavenly distance—eternal perspective. Trial eventually produces beauty, after the lessons have been learned, the temperaments have been refined, and Christlike attributes have been developed. Stepping back from the crude details allowed me to view my friend's house, and trial, differently—even as a scene of beauty. From a far-off perspective, the scene could very well be a magnificent castle set amidst pristine landscaping, where high in a tower a beautiful princess awaits rescue by a Prince of Peace, because from a distance—eternally—that's what the scene truly is.

Thanks, Bette.

26
A Day Late and a Dollop Short

A MODIFICATION OF THE WELL-KNOWN saying "a day late and a dollar short" to "a day late and a *dollop* short" is much more applicable to me because it is more comprehensive. I am frequently a day late and a dollar short, but additionally, I run short in so many other ways that I like to quantify them as "dollops."

In case you've heard that jingle, "Do a dollop of Daisy," and spent sleepless nights thinking of sour cream and asking, "What in the world is a dollop?" I offer you the definition before I begin my rant. *Dollop* (1) a lump or blob, as of paint or mud; (2) a small serving or portion (*The Random House Dictionary*, 1980; I'm a dollop short on updated dictionaries).

I am definitely a blob, lump, serving and/or portion short on brain cells, organization skills, parenting abilities, and social graces. In contrast, I am in excess of dollops on certain parts of my body, so the dollop, in all of its non-metric volume, is malicious either way. Anyway, I was definitely a dollop short one morning for parent day at my daughter's elementary school orchestra rehearsal.

I thought I'd better make a showing at this parent day since I'd ditched every other one before—dollop short. This was an invitation for parents to come observe the usual activities of orchestra rehearsal to help them, as quoted from the invitation, "increase understanding of what orchestra is all about and how to better encourage your child in practicing to increase effectiveness"(i.e., some of you are a dollop short on orchestra support and interest).

Orchestra is twice a week at 8:00 a.m., and I can pretty consistently manage to get my daughter there about seven minutes late. She has to get her honking huge cello out of the back of the van by herself because I'm usually wearing something that is publicly unacceptable—dollop short on morning hygiene and wardrobe. But I don't know why I worry since I never see anyone else dropping off their string-instrument-playing children seven minutes late.

I had big plans for this parent day though. I was going to get up and get all ready and be on time and not be a single dollop short. I had fantasies about my dazzling showing at parent day—until Tuesday morning, when I forgot it was parent day—dollop short. My daughter was downstairs getting ready, and I glanced at the calendar and noticed it read, "Orchestra Parent Day" at the top of the day I was looking at, which was the day that it was. It was now 7:52 a.m. on that day, which on a regular orchestra day would have been fine because we'd be right on track to be about seven minutes late. But it was parent day, and I didn't want to be seven minutes late, and I didn't want to be wearing ratty sweats and striped Christmas socks with Crocs and a family reunion T-shirt and my adult-onset acne uncovered—dollop short. In an effort to at least be less late than usual, I grabbed a coat and my daughter and made a run for it. We were maybe going to be only three and a half minutes late when my cell phone rang. It was my husband—"You forgot the cello."—dang dollop short!

In defeat, I went back for the cello, arrived twelve minutes late on parent day in ratty sweats, striped Christmas socks with Crocs, reunion T-shirt and adult-onset acne uncovered. I dropped my daughter off to give her some kind of head start while I parked the car . . . and also to save her from having to claim genetic connection to me. I would just sneak in the back unnoticed, hopefully.

Upon arriving in the orchestra room (which has no back entrance, which I did not know, being a parent day delinquent), I saw my daughter fumbling with her honking huge cello in a fluster to quickly join the group. There with her was an on-time, hygienically correct, well-dollop-endowed mother helping her. I ran to my daughter's aid and excused the orchestra EMT, trying to keep my morning breath downwind—dollop short.

We finally got situated and joined in the festivities. I tried not to notice other parents so I wouldn't have to torture myself with comparison. I tried not to notice the mother next to me with flawless hair, make-up, and a trendy outfit. I tried not to notice that not only had she gotten herself camera-ready and been on time with her orchestra student, but she also had three other young children in tow who sported gelled hair and Gap coordinates. I also tried not to notice other mothers who weren't wearing make-up—and didn't need to because they had clear skin.

Despite her parent, my daughter was not a dollop short on parent day. She knew every song by heart and was praised by her instructor for her technique. I even kicked up my striped Christmas socks and Crocs with her in a beat exercise dance. When it was all done, I helped pack up the honking huge cello, praised my sweet daughter, and thanked her for being seen with me on parent day. And then I headed home to find out what other dollops I'd be short on for the day.

27
My Odyssey to the Front of the Exercise Class

IN THE BEGINNING

It's 7:18 a.m. on the fifteenth day of January, and I've just returned from a 6:00 a.m. exercise class I've yet to be on time for. I've been attending this class faithfully, if not punctually, for two weeks in pursuit of keeping a New Year's resolution concerning my current body shape.

I read an inspiring tribute that should've made me feel honored to look like a walking kumquat. It went something like "The alterations to a woman's body as she selflessly brings children into the world stand as symbols of her sacrifice." Well, put me on an altar and light the kindling because every stretch-marked, sagging, cellulotic inch of my body screams sacrifice.

This goal is far from my first attempt. I have spent a fair share of my adult life trying to find the yellow brick road to my ideal body. I have simply lacked the discipline to get past Munchkinland. Thus, I've decided to take drastic measures.

I acquired a popular "healthy lifestyle" book. We don't say "diet" anymore because "it's not all about weight loss but forming new healthy lifestyle habits that help us confront our issues with food."

Whatever. I want to be a size four, and my issue with food is that I put too much of it in my face.

The book encouraged me to keep a journal to chart my progress. I am hoping that keeping a personal log of my attempt will create a sense of accountability and an obligation to actually pursue this resolution beyond Groundhog Day. If there must be written proof of my self-improvement efforts, I hope I can rise to the occasion and improve. Heaven forbid this becomes a sickening memoir of endless excuses for missed workouts and Oreo-shake fests.

So my journey has begun. Every weekday morning I fumble into the state-of-the-art exercise studio in my baggy shorts and stained T-shirt just late enough that I'll never completely recover the missed portion of the routine. I slouch on the back row with all the other non-matching workout wear people. I've settled into the class's unofficial hierarchy. The front row consists of the genetically blessed, never-miss-a-cue fitness freaks. Planted two feet from the wall-length mirror, these folks have no fear of the 8x10-foot glossy of themselves.

As the rows progress back, the energy-level notches go down, and the sweat-wear gets baggier and less color coordinated. I, currently serving as back row president, would rather die than stare at a life-size poster of myself prehygiene. Alas, as in any kingdom, the poor despise the rich because of envy.

I am a woman with big-boned excuses. I'm an active, sturdy Euro-stock girl with an appetite, a sweet tooth, and a couple pregnancies under my belt, literally. I'm not complaining. I'm grateful for the DNA hand I was dealt. I hail from a long line of sturdy people. I've never broken a bone, I have no allergies, and for these great blessings, I can overlook the fact that my ring size is larger than my husband's. I'm not a miracle diet psycho who thinks I can somehow transform my genetic codes into Barbiehood. I simply want to uncover the bod I know lurks somewhere under an ice cream addiction. I know that when next New Year's clock chimes, I'll be able to take my rightful place on the front row in my thong leotard.

Weight Training

Last week I collected on the complimentary personal trainer consultation that came with my new fitness club membership. I shopped for my trainer from the staff photos on the wall. From the moment I saw "Tony," I knew he was the one. I showed up for my appointment in the most matching outfit I could conglomerate and awaited to be taken under Tony's bulging wing. I was unaware that freebies are not multiple choice.

I was introduced to "Felice," who was so petite she could have worn my ring as an anklet. First, we sat down to evaluate my experience and set goals. I silently prayed I would not have to divulge my weight to Tinkerbell. Luckily, the interview was brief and painless, which was in direct contrast to the weight-training program she recommended. In summary, I did the fireman's crawl into the kitchen the next morning and sucked my cereal through a straw.

After six days of therapeutic massage, I braved the weight room on my own. With Felice's chart in hand, I headed to the intimidating free-weights section. It was "leg day," so I started with lunges. Two reps later, my legs were on fire. I couldn't wimp out in front of the surrounding hard bodies, so I toughed it out. After finishing the set, I tried to look casual as I frantically scanned my chart to double check the weight amount. I had put twenty-five pounds on each side of the bar, which, I discovered, was the amount for the next exercise. I was supposed to have done lunges with only the weight of the bar. That explained the severe cramping.

I completed my free-weights workout without further trauma and headed to the toning machines. I started on the inner and outer thigh machines, or "birthing chairs," as Felice affectionately called them—not that her hip size indicates any previous experience. I, however, looked right at home. I like the machines more than free weights. I've noticed there are always more women in this area. Men would rather pump iron and watch their muscles bulge in the mirror while they twist their faces in agony. I have seen men use the arm and back machines, but I have yet to witness any man on the birthing chairs.

Upon completion of my workout, I checked my legs to make sure they had not been amputated and replaced by pasta. I tried to walk out of the club with as much finesse as one can with no feeling below the waist. I practiced my fireman's crawl first thing when I got home so I'd be ready for breakfast in the morning.

Arm Day

Felice set up my schedule for two leg days and two arm days a week. She explained that after fatiguing muscles, I should rest those muscles for forty-eight hours. No argument. My legs still felt like they had herded cattle across Wyoming on horseback. I admit I was nervous about arm day. I sometimes get stiff after washing a hefty batch of dishes, and my triceps look more like a place to keep small change than muscles. Luckily, Felice arranged my arm workout on the machines. I couldn't bear the humiliation of struggling through biceps curls with my two-pound mini-bar next to He-Man as he casually bench-pressed 300 pounds.

I know I have a free-weights inferiority complex. I'm just intimidated by those who are confident doing free weights because I am not yet. I'm not just talking about men either. Believe me, there are seriously buff chicks who hold their own in free weights. The rest of us awkwardly muddle through one or two free-weight requirements and shuffle quickly back to the security blanket of the machines. I depend on those anatomically correct diagrams to show which muscles are supposed to be burning.

I finally realized why weight training intimidates me—I witnessed the frightening results of weight room cluelessness today. Those who enter the ironclad room in naïveté only bring shame to themselves. As I watched people mount benches in obscure ways and flail dumbbells aimlessly, I was thankful I at least had the decency to consult a professional first.

Weight room innocence reared its ugly head as I watched a waif mark eighty pounds on the lat pull-down apparatus. She saddled herself up on the way-too-high seat and attempted to maneuver the bar. After retching in pain for a few seconds, she managed to pull the bar even with her forehead. Then she made the mistake of breathing, which made her lose concentration, and the bar snapped back to the top of the machine, taking her with it. The abrupt jerk upward, accompanied by a loud crash, made her lose her grip, and she thumped back down onto the seat. She quickly dismounted and tried to look casual as she left the scene of the crime.

I find comfort in the security of the precious chart Felice made for me. I can only hope this mite of knowledge will spare me from anything that could cause serious damage to my budding weight room ego.

Weak-end

What is it about the word *weekend* that causes one to throw all caution to the wind? I must research the origin of this word because I know that in ancient translation it means "food free-for-all." A more accurate spelling of this word would be *w-e-a-k-e-n-d*. I have an array of adequate excuses to explain my spree. I'll relate a few of them for therapeutic balm.

First, my niece was having a sleepover with my daughter. What kind of aunt would I be if we didn't go to McDonald's Playland and have Happy Meals on Saturday afternoon? A video party complete with munchies, is a must. And then there was the birthday party on Sunday for my mom. If I didn't eat some of the cake I made, everyone would think I'd poisoned it.

Despite some indiscretions, this weekend actually showed tender buds of hope for me. I did an extra workout on Saturday, and at McDonald's, I ordered water and a grilled chicken sandwich. I scraped the mayo off the bun and snitched nary a fry. I did enjoy a kiddie cone, but I squelched the temptation to order an Oreo McFlurry, a major conquest for me. Such valiance will certainly make up for the tub of frosting I consumed while decorating my mom's birthday cake.

Joining the Bod Squad

I succumbed to buying matching athletic wear. I know I mocked people who spend good money on clothes to sweat in, but I have come to understand what motivates such a purchase.

I had to exercise nearer to the front last week due to my tardiness and the excessive number of back-rowers. As I was forced to view a larger image of myself in the mirror, I realized that hiding behind oversized rags does little for my self-esteem or motivation level. My current figure does have a few good sides, none of which are flattered in a toga.

As I glanced around the room, I noticed it was not just those with Greek physiques who sweat color-coordinatedly. There is an emerging population working toward their goals in style. They've stepped out of their tunics, moved off the back row, and are challenging the space between them and the mirror. Although these middle-class folks in our kingdom were not born into the beautiful-bod elite, their determination spurs them on to rise above their station in life.

I realized my denial to invest in new workout wear stems from the reasoning that I'll indulge in new clothes when I fit into smaller sizes. As I slump on the back row in my ratty T-shirt and glance longingly at those more fortunate, I only plant my feet deeper into bod poverty.

So I decided to acquaint myself with the world of sportswear. I carefully surveyed the superstore selection that featured everything from parachute pants to neon thongs. My quest was to find a combination that would emphasize the good and hide the bad until it gets better. I am what smug glamour magazine analysts categorize as a "Pear—small top, large bottom." I found some sporty fitted tops to emphasize my smaller top then shopped for something to camouflage the bulging portion of the pear. I perused the shorts but went for sleek, dark sweatpants, since I suffer from knee-load syndrome and I admit to being an infrequent shaver.

As I assessed the metamorphosis in the dressing room mirror, I felt like a new woman. I felt leaner as I admired the way these clothes smoothed out the rough edges. I stepped out of the tent and found out I had a figure with promise. So I proudly joined the workforce in class today, sporting my new clothes and confidence. This small but significant investment helped me leave the confinements of self-doubt behind and gain a few steps on my voyage.

Judgment Day

I suppose a progress report is due. Some might think it grotesque to pull out a tape measure and calculate progress in the buff. I personally find it much more motivating to chart the actual shrinkage of my thighs over time than to stand on the scale in fear and trembling. To date, I've lost a total of two and seven-eighths inches. Even my lower body is starting to shed bulges I thought would never budge.

Speaking of bulges, I should mention that at the start of this goal, I did the unthinkable—I put on a swimsuit and made my husband take one of those awful "before" photos. Of course, I gave my best gorilla stance and left my hair and make-up undone to further emphasize the ugliness. If all else fails, I can at least do my hair and make-up for the "after" photo and look better in some respect. My figure can be forgiving in clothes, but when I saw the photo, I wretched in pain. I pitied the one-hour photo lab worker who was forced to develop it for a mere minimum wage pittance.

I've heard the analysis of how anorexics think they look fat no matter how thin they are. I have the reverse of this problem; maybe it's called anti-rexia. When I look in the mirror, no matter how bad it's getting, I still think I'm staying above the curve. When I see an unflattering vacation photo of myself I think the camera had a distortion problem. But there was no hiding in this photo. There was the half-naked truth in living color. The good news is that this self-inflicted torture did increase my motivation.

Holy Flu-bug, Batman!

I made it on time to class Monday morning to begin the month with new commitment, since the last week of January showed slack. I started feeling achy and groggy but dismissed it as being tired from the weekend. When the alarm went off the next morning, I was already awake due to a nagging headache. Still in denial, I got up and started to get ready. When I leaned over to tie my shoes, the full force of the flu set in—fever, chills, aches, cough, congestion, the whole Nyquil nine yards. The rest of the week was basically a blur of pain and mucus.

Though still nursing a hacking cough, I am feeling much better. I'm actually anxious to get back to the gym, though I think that's where I picked up this bug. There are always folks wheezing through their workouts. I used to look at such people and wonder why they didn't bask in the excuse for missing a few days, but now I understand this obsessive behavior.

Even on the days I wouldn't have been startled to see my own lung surface during a cough bout, I would be planning to do a make-up workout later if I felt better. I think the root of this insanity is the fear that missing a few days will cause my body to coagulate back into curds.

Low Blow

Reading back through my last entry activated my gag reflex. The fling with the flu certainly knocked the wind out of my sails. Every morning when my alarm goes off, I feel like someone must have welded my behind to the bed in the night. It also feels like two in the morning since it is still so dark outside.

Maybe it's the eight new inches of snow and twenty-degree temperature drop this week that pushed me into the depths of winter despair. The Groundhog is a traitor and a coward! He peeks out of his hole, dashes our hopes with a smirk and a shadow, and then retires to the warmth and security of hibernation.

Despite my current motivation disorder, I have managed to go three for three so far this week. Today was the first day I went to class though. I've been doing the treadmill instead. I was afraid if the instructor was overly peppy, I might lose it and take her down. A cheery pixie bouncing through her catchy choreography was beyond my tolerance threshold. I just wanted to sweat in peace and be alone with my bad attitude.

I'm not the only one suffering from winter blues. The class that is usually busting at the seams was sparse today, and the gym overall has been less populated. People seem to trudge through their workouts, lowering the incline on the treadmill, taking longer breaks between sets. But we're sticking it out! We may be hatin' it right now, but we'll have the last laugh when swimsuit season hits, right?

This is the time of year that separates the men from the boys. New Year's resolutions start to fade in memory, the winter drags eternally on, and only the truly dedicated thwart the desire to let go. Sure, everybody will perk up in a few weeks when the sun starts teasing through the clouds and glamour magazines release spring preview issues. Tan, toned bodies wallpaper the newsstands and remind us of the lumps that have been lurking under layers of wool since Christmas. Then everybody laces up their cross trainers and becomes fitness gurus. But the few, the proud, the insane, duke it out with Old Man Winter and beat the bulge by six weeks. Just when everyone else resumes motivation, we are down to fine-tuning.

Do I know what I'm talking about? Not a clue. Am I saying all this to make myself feel better? Definitely. Is it working? Sort of. It sounds good, doesn't it? If in six weeks I can put on a swimsuit and smile, or at least restrain tears, I will personally go on a crusade promoting the value of dedication. If not, I will disclaim the self-discipline dribble in this journal, sponsor a healthy-lifestyle book-burning, and preach eat, drink, and be merry.

For now, I've got to be strong. This is when I usually give up, and I have to make it this time. I have to see if it can be done, and if it can, will it be worth it? My deep yearning to know the answers to these disturbing questions is the only thing that has neutralized the chemical bond between my mattress and me each morning.

In the wise words of Yoda, "Do or do not. There is no try."

Regression

I've been avoiding my journal due to shame. The stock market took a dive this week, and I went down with it. I've basically been a binge basketcase.

It all started on Valentine's Day; I had a torrid and tainted love affair with a double batch of sugar cookies. We hooked up in the garage with the freezer door still open.

I originally intended to treat my family for the holiday then freeze the extra batch for future resource. It was stupid to think I would be able to divert my thoughts from available goodies. I have a wicked sweet tooth, and I am terrible at rebuffing a craving.

This reveals my most self-destructive cycle. After a pitfall, I decide that since I've already blown it, I'll just bask in my shame for the remainder of the week (month, season, etc.) and start anew at a later date. Then I proceed to stuff my face at will until my new starting day comes. I gladly renew my resolve until I have another pitfall; then it starts all over again.

I managed to conquer a grueling week of plummeting exercise motivation, I controlled a fit of withdrawal when I passed the candy at a Super Bowl party, and I can't remember the last time I had an Oreo shake, which is my medicinal, universal fix-all. And yet, one batch of cookies set into motion the cycle that explains my unsuccessful career in size management.

Recovery

It's always darkest just before dawn, and luckily dawn cracked in the nick of time. I managed to salvage my progress and have even made some headway. The cottage cheese on my legs is even starting to de-curd. I credit my comeback to this journal. Writing about the dark secrets lurking behind my cellulite has been educational. I never realized what a psycho I was.

The prediction I made during the lull in gym attendance was right on. Over the past two weeks, the once-abandoned gym has quickly evolved into a nest of worried wasps. Swimsuits are out on the racks, and everybody is dialing it up a notch to make up for lost time. I have to wait for machines or work in with others to get through my workout. Annoying. I've established seniority over this bunch of fair-weather friends. Sure, now that it's lighter and warmer outside, they think they can just come in and take over. Well, what they don't realize is that while they were away, a weight-room weed bloomed.

I used to be ever-so quiet, replacing weights on the rack in fear that the least bit of noise might indicate my presence. Now I clang and bang all I want. I even grunted once. I've bonded with the weight room. Dare I call myself a gym rat? Those dark, lonely weeks in the weight room gave me the opportunity to find my feet. Now the crowd is back, and I feel an invasion of my territory. But I've decided to share my domain. I suppose there is room for everyone.

Further proof of my blossoming relationship with the gym is that I am now the proud owner of a locker. Actually, I'm a tenant, not an owner. For a mere five dollars a month, I've established semi-permanent residence at number 268, Women's Locker Room. I was in junior high again as I filled my locker with personal toiletries. I forgot my hunk poster, but all in due time. It's liberating to go to the gym free from the hassle of bags and bottles. After a hard workout, I skip to the locker room, knowing that everything I need to scrub and buff is ready and waiting. I feel liberated! Setbacks promote growth. Spring is truly the season of renewal.

Neglect

It's been hit-and-run lately. This crazy month has truly been a test of my dedication to this goal. I've managed to do at least four workouts a week, but it has been haphazard.

This month I've been sluffing my bedtime in a vain effort to whittle away at my to-do list. My moonlighting made it difficult to get up early, and when my workout started pushing eight o'clock, I had to start going in the evening so as not to corrupt the entire workday.

I hate going in the evening. It's crowded, and there's a whole different atmosphere. Early morning people want to work out and get out. We have chosen the early workout because we are dedicated (desperate) to squeeze fitness into our already overstuffed lives. We go about our workouts in an impersonal, systematic manner because we have a life to get back to as quickly as possible. The evening crowd is a whole different breed. The gym transforms into a hangout.

The evening crowd is full of singles and teenyboppers who seize the opportunity to wear spandex and mingle. Chat circles form on the mats, and machines fill up with yakking groupies. I try being patient by altering my workout according to availability, but when it gets ridiculous, I apply my best annoyed hover.

There's no one to blame but myself for getting off schedule, and I have found observing the creative mix of mating patterns and machines to be quite entertaining. It must take these people hours to actually complete a workout, if that's what they really come for.

The evening crowd does have superior aesthetics to the morning crowd. Perhaps the reason a.m. people keep to themselves is that most of us haven't brushed our teeth yet. The p.m. folks are coming from work or school, so their grooming is still intact. I've watched girls apply make-up and fluff hair in the locker room before starting their workout. This deepens my suspicions about their true motive.

Hygiene neglect of the a.m. exerciser does have a purpose. One of the great beauties of the morning workout is to get the sweat session over with while already covered with residue and then clean up for the day.

Alas, I reconverted this morning to the early workout. If I don't go in the morning, I worry all day that I'm not going to have the time or energy to go. Early mornings can be brutal at times, but when the day starts to slip into overdrive it is exhilarating to note that my workout is already behind me. Well, it's getting late, and I'd best be heading to bed so I can reclaim my early bird status.

Swan Thong

I did not reclaim early bird status. I wish my motivation to regroup came from the excitement of wanting to record a petite new clothing size. Actually, I can report a new clothing size, but it's far from petite—it's maternity. The "before" and "after" photos will definitely show a change. Not exactly the rally I thought I was going to have. I suppose this goal was an attempt to get a few bulges under control before I made some more. Foiled again.

People say that a woman glows when she's pregnant. I hate to mar that lovely thought by revealing that the glow is really grease from the fried chicken bucket she just licked clean. In the end, as the clock ticks on, gravity pulls down, metabolism gears lose lube, so losing is a losing battle in the end, right? (No healthy lifestyle book is going to pick up that quote from this journal.) On a positive note, my protruding girth will buffer the view of how fat my legs get over the next several months.

Maybe I'll be bold and uninhibited during this pregnancy, like Demi. As a farewell tribute to my New Year's resolution and completion of my odyssey, I'll march (waddle) proudly to the front of my class wearing a maternity thong leotard.

28
Church Volleybrawl

I WOULD LIKE TO BEAR testimony that the Church sports program is true comedy. People have left the Church because of Church ball. People have come into the Church because of Church ball. People have permanently lost lifelong friends and the use of appendages because of Church ball.

Something strange happens when so-called Saints put on jerseys and try to recapture their youth in the church gymnasium. We say a prayer: "Please help us to have good sportsmanship and keep us safe from harm or injury." Then we pound on each other.

One doomed weekend, I managed to get caught in the middle of some Church ball drama. I was put in charge of our stake women's volleyball team for the regional tournament. My friend was the stake athletic director and asked me to act as the team coach for her since she couldn't be there. I'm no superstar, but I did play a couple years in high school, so I know my way around the court. We had some serious players on our team, including a former high school coach, so it's not like anyone needed my pointers or anything. I was just supposed to organize our team, fill out our lineup sheet, etc. Easy enough . . . or so I thought.

When I got there, I picked up a lineup sheet and began filling it out. I had barely put a pencil to the paper when I was quickly maneuvered out of the process by a couple of highly skilled and very competitive team members. We had eight women for the six positions, so we would need to substitute in order to give everyone play time. I noticed these two "sweet sisters" made sure they were not subs the first couple games. I didn't think much of it at first since I knew their skills and knowledge of the game exceeded mine, so I let them do their thing. But game after game went by without them ever being subs, and those they apparently felt were inferior players spent more and more time warming the bench. I started to get bugged. I don't know why I am always naïve enough to trust that grown people understand how life works.

This was Church ball, for heaven's sake! These women came to get out of the house to have some fun, get away from their kids, and get a little exercise. All the ladies on our team had some high school ball experience and were solid players, but even if not, everyone deserved equal play time.

Before the next game, I tried to work my way back into the lineup process. I approached it casually at first: "So we should probably make the play time a little more equal, and those who haven't subbed *at all* yet need to take their turn this game, okie dokie?"

"Yeah, yeah," they said, not looking up as they hovered more closely over the lineup sheet.

They set it up so they did sub out, but only for the back row part of the rotation; then they would come back in to rule the net. Everyone knows playing the front row is the most fun. It's where all the action is. It's where you get to slam it down someone's throat, strategically dink it over their block, or shove their own net tricks back in their face.

I know the Twin Towers thought they were being so generous to grant us half of their precious rotation, but they were not Gladys Knight, and we weren't just their back row Pips. And it's not like they played without making mistakes. Their mistakes may have been cooler, like spiking so hard or serving so long that the ball went out of bounds, but a lost point is a lost point whether it's a spastic dig or an overshot spike. They were also mega ball hogs. They played about three positions at a time, which caused collisions and missed plays because of confusion over other people wanting to touch the ball sometimes too.

When they were on the back row, they still played like they were on the front, setting to each other for spikes instead of utilizing the front row players. If you were on the front row with them, they forced the funky switch thing after the serve to get the position they wanted. When someone got in their way or missed a shot they thought they would've had, their disdain was obvious. I shook my head at the display. I didn't want to make a scene, but I kept trying to subtly put in my two bits about the situation, hoping they'd clue in. They swatted me away like a pesky fly.

By the end of the night, I'd had it. I apologized to the ladies who had gotten benched the most and told them to please, please come back the next day to play out the rest of the tournament. The next morning, I had about decided to ditch. I figured one less player would at least reduce the subbing issue, and the team hardly needed me to act as coach since the Twin Towers obviously had things covered.

Then a friend who usually plays for the team but couldn't come the night before called to see if she could get in on the game. I gave her the scoop and told her she could go in my place if she wanted to but to remember I gave her fair warning.

She said, "It surprises me they bulldozed you. You're not usually one to back down."

She was right. What was I doing? I'm no marshmallow! I'm a tough broad whose bark is nothing compared to my bite when necessary. Plus, I was given official jurisdiction as coach, and I was ready to lay the smack down. This was more than just a Church ball game now. This was a fight between right and wrong, good and evil. We were women in the gospel who deserved equal share of play time, dang it!

I arrived early and had the lineup sheet all filled out and turned in. When everyone arrived, I explained that as "the official coach" I would do the game lineups, and everyone would sub equally. The Twin Towers started to protest, to which I replied, "You two got mad skills, but this is Church ball, and we all came to play so you *will* take your turn substituting like the rest of us. Capiche?"

They were stunned. How dare I challenge their bossiness with counter bossiness? We all knew I didn't have any real jurisdiction. We're a bunch of frumpy moms in sweats regurgitating our high school volleyball skills for kicks in a Church gym on a Saturday morning to put off chores. But apparently the Twin Towers finally reached their petty limit. Perhaps they realized the only thing more pathetic than being Church ball divas was to defend their right to be Church ball divas.

We made it all the way to the championship that morning. We lost the final game, but another victory was won at a Church athletic event that day. Right prevailed. Fairness was preserved. Compromise was accomplished. And an alpha female got her groove back.

About the Author

As a community blogger for the *Herald Journal* news, frequent LDS media contributor, and author, Kari J. Rich enjoys exposing the hidden hilarity that lurks in everyday life. She is a mother of three, wife of Western artist Jason Rich, and resident of the outback of Cache Valley, Utah, with more animals than she ever wanted to take care of. Kari likes to read, bike, design, and quilt when she's not loading the dishwasher.

She graduated from Utah State University in English and design and worked in an advertising agency and as a freelancer in copywriting and design. She has written for radio and has done professional writing and concepting for numerous commercial companies. Follow more of Kari's writing at kari-on. com.

Kari believes laughter is the best medicine, which is a good thing because she doesn't have very good health insurance.